John the Baptist

John the Baptist

by

CARL H. KRAELING

CHARLES SCRIBNER'S SONS, NEW YORK

CHARLES SCRIBNER'S SONS, LTD., LONDON

1951

TO THE COLLEAGUES

OF THE

DIVINITY SCHOOL OF YALE UNIVERSITY

AND OF THE

OBERLIN GRADUATE SCHOOL OF THEOLOGY

Contents

Foreword

AT no time, it would seem, has anyone doubted that
John the Baptist is a figure of outstanding importance for our knowledge of later Judaism and of the beginnings of Christianity. Jesus and the Evangelists thought
so and modern writers on Gospel story have continued to
emphasize the fact. In the course of the twenty years during which it was my privilege to teach at the Divinity
School of Yale University the basic course on the Life and
Teaching of Jesus, I had recurrently the opportunity to
wish for a small book in the English language that would
set forth what modern scholarship felt it could say about
John, his preaching, his rite and his influence upon contemporaries and succeeding generations. Such books existed or were coming into print in French and German,
but in English we had only older monographs, seriously
dated, or introductory chapters in the traditional type of
the Life of Jesus that were insufficient in scope. At the same
time, practical experience showed that to study what the

sources say about John provided an excellent opportunity
to learn and to teach the procedures of historical criticism,
simplifying and paving the way for their application to
the material dealing with Jesus. When, therefore, I was
invited to deliver the Haskell Lectures at the Oberlin
Graduate School of Theology in 1946, I was happy indeed
not only to serve in so distinguished a capacity, but also
to try to supply a practical need so long felt. The lectures
are published substantially as delivered, with only such
notes as seemed absolutely necessary.

Additional information about religious movements in
the Judaism of the immediately pre-Christian period is
just beginning to emerge from the study of the Dead Sea
Scrolls. At a few points it promises to enrich our knowledge of the background against which John's life and work
developed, but does not change or effect radically the picture here presented.

Those elements of the presentation that deal with contemporary political and cultural conditions are the by-
product of a continuing preoccupation with the archaeo-
logical materials of the Near East and their interpretation.
Those that bear upon Judaism derive largely from the
highly profitable study of the *haggadah* begun in connection with my work on the Dura Synagogue paintings.
Those, finally, that are of a methodological nature and
exhibit my understanding of the procedures necessary to
the proper use of Gospel material, I owe to my beloved
teacher, the late Professor Martin Dibelius of the University of Heidelberg, Germany. These last require a word of
explanation for the general reader.

It will be evident from the lectures that I think of the

Gospels as embodying the substance of an oral tradition composed ultimately of individual narratives and sayings. As orally transmitted, these units of material gave only the scantiest and most general information about the circumstances under which an event occurred and normally no information at all about the particular context in which a given saying was uttered, thus often leaving historical value and meaning open to question. Moreover, the units reach us in a variety of forms resulting partly from their passage through written sources and partly from the vicissitudes of the oral transmission itself. To determine their value and meaning we cannot fall back in the first instance upon dogma, upon the supposed personal connection between a given Evangelist and a given eye-witness or Apostle, upon theories of the filiation of documents or upon dialectical method. Rather, we must interpret the material in the light of what we can infer about the process of its own transmission. This means asking the stories and sayings to tell us first about the persuasions, the interests, the problems and the conflicts of those who transmitted them. This we can properly do since it is clear that most of what was remembered, and thus ultimately written down in our sources, had some practical relevance for those who cherished and transmitted the information, the variant renderings giving particularly valuable clues to changing attitudes and points of view in the chain of transmission.

To say that the separate relevance of the units of Gospel material to the religious and practical life of the informants is an essential guide to their proper interpretation and evaluation, is to subscribe to Dibelius' principle of the *Sitz im Leben* (relation to contemporary life). The principle, systematically applied here to a small body of material, throws into sharp relief the fact that the Synoptic Gospels are among the best and the least-used sources for the history of the Christian and Baptist movements in Palestine and Syria during the first two generations of their development. It also emphasizes the dynamic and persuasive character of the Baptist and Christian movements, indicating that at their core lies not a set of inflexible intellectual stereotypes but an element of lasting commitment and of personal relationship. If the application of the principle has served not only to clarify the historical figure of the Baptist, but also to enhance his tremendous power and vitality, these lectures will have served a twofold purpose.

CARL H. KRAELING

Sometime Buckingham Professor of New Testament Criticism and Interpretation in Yale University, Director of the Oriental Institute of the University of Chicago

I

John the Baptist and the Wilderness

THE century between Pompey's reorganization of the Near East in 63 B.C. and the Revolt against Rome in 66–71 A.D. is a period of momentous importance in the life of the Jewish people and one of unusual interest to the historian. In the pattern of its development the period is highly complicated, for virtually every aspect of Jewish life was caught up during some part of the time in the broader current of world affairs and directly affected by it. The century saw great forces clashing with each other in Palestine and circumstances conspiring to make adjustment to pressures from this side and that extremely difficult. The basic conflict, of course, was that between the principles and practices of Roman rule and the institutions and ideals of the Jewish nation as a sovereign people under God. Equally important, however, were the tensions created in the social and economic sphere. Here the conflict centered about the ambitious program of

1

urbanization and of capitalistic enterprise by which the Herodians sought to bring a relatively simple and self-sufficient agrarian Palestine into line with the highly industrial and urban civilization of the Augustan era. In the field of religious life and thought, too, there was turmoil, as opportunism on the one side and escape from reality on the other, working at cross purposes with the desire for individual acceptability before God through pious observance, created factions and antipathies, threatening with destruction the unity of the one Holy People.

What the sources have to tell us about the complicated interplay of these larger forces is the natural focus of the historian's interest. Yet his narrative would lack much of its fascination did it not include also some account of the individual personalities that move across the stage of history in the period, moulding the course of events and moulded, in turn, by it. A simple roster of this personnel has about it all the variety of a Shakespearean *dramatis personæ*. It embraces, on the one hand, triumvirs, emperors, governors, half-caste vassal kings, tetrarchs, adventurers and adventuresses, and a host of minor civil and military officials. On the other hand, it includes priestly aristocrats and their unpretentious landed colleagues, a galaxy of scholars and saints, various sectaries, dreamers, demagogues and fanatics, not to mention soberminded burghers and judges of the people. No less fascinating than any of these is a modest company of individuals through whom, by a significant inversion, the self-criticizing, self-correcting tendency of the Hebrew genius reasserted itself as so often under similar circumstances in the past. Like the Prophets of old, these men spoke with the assurance of divine inspiration words of warning and comfort to a world in which the current of human affairs threatened to undermine the spiritual foundations of national and individual life. Prophet-like they were swept aside in the hurly-burly of the day, but prophet-like they did not cease to haunt men in the inner recesses of the mind.

To this modest company of individuals we must assign a certain John, commonly called "the Baptist," whose person and proclamation injected themselves ominously into the pattern of Jewish religious and political life in the late twenties of the first century of our era. Many of those in higher places regarded him as dangerous, a demonic force disturbing men's minds and retarding the wheels of progress. Many of the common people of his day found him not only provocative but compelling, so much so that for almost a decade after his violent death the question of his vindication was a popular issue. For some centuries the rite he performed was bartered about and imitated in sundry syncretistic religious communities of the Near East, and in Christianity and in one non-Christian, non-Jewish sect he has played a continuous role down to the present day. This makes him a person of significance in his own right and an excellent medium for the study of the period to which he belonged. In this capacity he deserves well at the hands of students of the New Testament, better, in fact, than he has received in

3

America and England, where no monograph devoted entirely to him has appeared for some years.[1]* It is with the thought of remedying, somewhat, our deficiency at this point that this study of the man whom the early Christians called "the Voice in the Wilderness" is undertaken.

The material available for our study of John is limited. Most of the early evidence comes from Christian documents contained in the New Testament, from Mark, from the Second Source, from Matthew, Luke, Acts and John, and consists of stories about John, words of John, stories about Jesus in which John appears, sayings of Jesus that deal with John, and simple items of factual information handed down as common knowledge without reference to specific narratives or sayings.[2] To this New Testament material we can add a single paragraph about the Baptist in the eighteenth book of the *Antiquities* which the Jewish historian Josephus composed about 93–94 A.D.[3] This evidence is not only meager but comes from what we know as "secondary" sources. This means that it has to be used with great caution to allow for the particular point of view from which the Christian writers on the one side and a man of Josephus' Pharisaic orientation on the other approached the figure of the Baptist. At the outset it would seem, therefore, that the limitations far outweigh the promise of the subject.

Conscious of these limitations, some have in more recent years tried to overcome them by introducing other later materials—the so-called Slavonic Josephus, and the

*Notes will be found at the back of the book.

documents of the Mandeans, an ancient Gnostic sect still surviving near Baghdad whose members call themselves "disciples of John"—or by discovering beneath the surface of the New Testament documents the remains of a written Baptist "literature" supposedly used by the Biblical Evangelists.[4] No one of these attempts to provide supplementary information or to enhance the significance of certain of the Biblical data can be said to have been entirely successful. There is important material in both the "Slavonic" Josephus, so-called, and in the Mandean writings, but it appears to contribute directly only to our knowledge of Baptist legend in the later, medieval period. That there may have been a Baptist "literature" in the period of the early Church is entirely possible, but the specific suggestions of its use by the Evangelists are unconvincing or rest on the most tenuous hypotheses. The chances are that whatever the New Testament writers knew about John came by word of mouth into the tradition which their informants handed on to them.[5]

Thrown back as we are, therefore, upon what others than his own sympathizers have written about John, we are by no means left entirely in the dark by virtue of this fact. When all due allowance has been made for Josephus' blind spots on the one side, and for the attempts of the Evangelists to capture John for the Christian Gospel on the other, it still remains true that these writers or their informants were his countrymen, and that in Christian circles, if anywhere, the basis for the preservation of a valid historical tradition about him may be said to have existed. This follows not only from the similarity of the movements begun by Jesus and John, but also from the relation of the two men to each other and from an early period of fraternization between Christian believers and Baptist disciples, a period during which there was apparently ample opportunity for Jesus' followers to become acquainted with reminiscences of John's converts. To obtain a valid and vivid picture of the Baptist what we need is not more new evidence but a better understanding of the way to read the available New Testament sources. Here we have to modify, somewhat, the procedure followed by the great Liberals of the nineteenth century.

Starting from the tacit assumption that the roots of significant religious movements are ideological in character, these men endeavored to abstract from the Biblical documents an element of residual fact, casting aside as useless all that pious imagination and theological reflection had added to the record. Applying this principle they eventually reduced even Jesus himself to a teacher of ethics whose entire wisdom could be summed up in a combination of the Golden Rule and the two greatest commandments in the Law. Starting from the observation that the materials of religious tradition are expressions of the life of religious communities, we today affirm that great religious movements are dynamic in character, reflecting the impact of powerful personalities upon successive generations of followers. This impact is often as clearly revealed in what men imagined and believed about such personalities as in what they knew about them. Everything we read in the New Testament about Jesus and John is therefore of some evidential value. Our problem is to interpret the material in such a way as to obtain not only elements of residual fact but also impressions of the forces unleashed, forces sufficiently strong to explain the further development of the tradition. Reading the available material in this way we discover that it yields a vivid picture of John as one who stirred mightily generations of pious Jews in the first century of our era.

When John first comes directly into our field of vision he is a grown man who haunts the desert places. The fact of this, his wilderness sojourn, is undeniable, for it has the support of the entire Christian tradition and is a necessary presupposition of much of the early comment he elicited, both favorable and unfavorable.[6] Luke 1:80 and later Baptist legend have the wilderness sojourn begin in John's infancy. This is intrinsically improbable and serves largely to fill a blank period in earlier accounts of his life.[7] Yet it testifies at the same time to the positive importance which the desert had for the understanding of his character and mission in the mind of his friends and followers.

What the Evangelists and Jesus meant when they spoke of John as "appearing" in the "desert" or the "wilderness" is perfectly clear. The term *eremos* which they used consistently in this connection describes not a region of shifting sands, as we might infer from the trans-

lation "desert," or a forest, as we might infer from the
translation "wilderness," but rather a solitary place, an
area devoid of human life and of the evidences of human
occupation, agricultural or otherwise. This, the Hebrew
equivalent *midbar* and the Hieronymian rendering *soli-
tudo* clearly reflect. In the New Testament the word
eremos can, therefore, be used of the place where the
shepherd pastures his flocks (in the Parable of the Lost
Sheep, Lk 15:4), as well as of the place where the crowds
who have followed Jesus find it impossible to obtain food
(in the story of the Multiplication of the Loaves, Mk
6:35).

There are large stretches of such uninhabited and
uninhabitable land in southern Palestine even today—
the craggy barren hilltops of the uplands, the declivitous,
deeply-fissured slopes of the Judæan massif and the inland
plateau, and finally the gently sloping detritus waste and
the alluvial plain of the Jordan valley and the Dead Sea
basin. Only two New Testament writers offer any suggestion as to the particular section of it that John may
be thought to have haunted. The one is Matthew, who
says that John came preaching in the "wilderness of
Judæa" (3:1). In traditional Hebrew usage, the "wilderness of Judæa" is the area along the eastern shore of the
Dead Sea where John certainly could not have baptized.
Matthew has apparently used the designation loosely,
thereby reducing its value for us.[8] The other is the Fourth
Evangelist, who gives us two place names associated with
John's activity, namely, Bethany across the Jordan and

Ænon near Salim (Jn 1:28, cf. 10:40, and Jn 3:23).
Archæological exploration on the one hand and a study
of patristic evidence on the other has now generally
clarified the location of these two sites. Bethany, with
its variant Bethabara, is probably a hamlet on the eastern
side of the Jordan not far from the place where the river
was forded by those traveling the main highway from
Jerusalem eastward by way of Jericho to Rabbath Am-
mon in Transjordan. Adjacent to the spring or the wells
of the *Wadi el-Kharrar,* it lay in what was ancient Peræa
and belonged thus to the territory of Herod Antipas, a
fact which it is important to remember. Ænon, meaning
"springs," is almost certainly the designation of a well-
watered area some thirty miles up the Jordan valley on
the western bank of the stream. It lay north even of the
latitude of the city of Samaria, not far from the place
where the highway leading northward from Jerusalem
dipped down into the Jordan valley before passing Scy-
thopolis (*Beisan*) and thus reaching the Lake of Galilee.[9]

Of the value of these place names for our knowledge
of John's wilderness sojourn there is corroborative testimony in the fact that the Baptist was taken prisoner by
Herod Antipas, which must have happened in Peræa, and
in the fact that while the strength of John's movement
lay in the district of Judæa, the faithful of Galilee found
him within their reach.[10]

More important than what they tell us about the
range of the territory covered, is what these place names
tell us about the nature of John's wilderness sojourn. If

9

John baptized near Bethany across Jordan and at Ænon near Salim, it follows that though he lived in the wilderness, he did not immobilize himself in anchorite fashion, and that, though he avoided human habitations, he was never remote from the important highways upon which men traveled north and south and east and west. To allow for such mobility and accessibility on John's part is not to make him an itinerant preacher as Luke has done (3:3) in his effort to accommodate him to the pattern of Christian missionary enterprise. It is, however, to recognize that John's wilderness sojourn did not have eremitic seclusion as its sole or dominant purpose. Even in the wilderness John permitted, and even encouraged, people to find him.

Early tradition has supplied us with two details concerning John's life in the wilderness, his food of locusts and wild honey, and his garment of camel's hair (Mk 1:6). The importance of these details has been greatly developed and exaggerated, particularly in later Byzantine legend. Perhaps the earliest stage of this exaggerating development is to be found in the Infancy Narrative where the angel Gabriel says of the unborn John, "wine and fermented liquor he will not drink" (Lk 1:15). What is implied here is that John's abstinence is of a Nazirite type and that by virtue of his dietary program he can lay claim to an unusual measure of sanctity.

Except for the fact that it is specific, there is nothing in Mark's statement about John's food that could be construed as involving a special dietary program. Locusts

10

and "wild honey," whether the latter was an animal or a vegetable product, were both familiar foods in ancient Palestine and were permitted by Jewish dietary laws.[11] But they did not sanctify those who consumed them. Indeed, we have a saying of Jesus which implies that in John's own day his diet was regarded as anything but sacred in its associations. This is the familiar word, "John came neither eating nor drinking and they say he has a demon" (Mt 11:18; Lk 7:33). The meaning of the statement turns on the interpretation of the expression "to have a demon" (*echein daimonion*). Usually this expression is taken to imply that the person in question is "possessed by a demon," so that he does what the demon says, and for this interpretation support can be found in the Fourth Gospel for instance, where Jesus accuses the Jews of being the children of Satan and they reply, "Say we not well that thou art a Samaritan and hast a demon" (Jn 8:48). The Synoptic Evangelists, however, when they wish to refer to a man possessed by a demon use the expression *daimonizomenos*. What they mean when instead they say *echein daimonion* we can see from the Beelzebub controversy, where the scribes explain Jesus' exorcisms by saying, "He hath Beelzebub, and by the prince of the demons casteth he out the demons" (Mk 3:22). When the scribes say that Jesus "has the demon Beelzebub" they clearly do not mean that Jesus is in the power of the prince of the demons, for otherwise Jesus could not be thought to bring any pressure upon the lesser demons through their prince. Rather the thought is that Jesus, "having the demon Beelzebub," actually has him under his power so that he can make him do as he wishes, namely, in this instance order his lesser minions to desist.[12] It is probable that the same meaning attaches to the expression "he has a demon" in the statement about the Baptist. The thought is not that John is possessed by a demon but that he has a demon under his control who must do as John tells him. The relevance of this interpretation for Jesus' word about John becomes clear when we grasp the nature of the problem that John's removal to the wilderness presented. The question was how, if he separated himself from the normal sources of food supply, he could manage to survive. The same question posed itself over and over again in connection with the sojourn of prophets in the wilderness. In the case of Elijah, the pious said that God sent him food by the ravens, and in the case of Jesus, the believers said that the angels came and ministered to him. Jesus would probably have said something similar about John, but John's enemies contended instead that John had a demon under his control whom he could command to bring him food whenever he wished, quite as Aladdin could order the genie of the lamp to spread a meal before him at his pleasure.

The general meaning of Jesus' statement, "the Son of Man came eating and drinking and they say, Behold a glutton and a wine-bibber, and John came neither eating nor drinking and they say, He hath a demon," is this. There are no aspects of the life of God's ministers which cannot be turned against them given enough animosity on the part of the interpreters. One would think, Jesus means to say, that John's being able to survive in the wilderness would have convinced people that he was under God's protection, but instead his enemies said he survived by using black magic. That being so, Jesus says, my own failure to withdraw into the wilderness cannot but bring against me the charge that I cater too much to my own stomach to be God's spokesman. We all recognize the "open and shut" type of argumentation by which scoffers, giving heed only to superficial contrasts, could escape from the necessity of any commitment. For our immediate purposes, however, it follows only that the food of which John did partake, namely, locusts and "wild honey," cannot have been regarded *a priori* as having any sanctifying character. Otherwise, the charge of its being supplemented by demonic assistance could not have arisen.

There is, then, in the earliest tradition, no tangible basis for the later view that John was observing the sanctifying dietary regimen of the Nazirite.[13] What is said about his food is to be taken merely as an attempt to characterize his life in the wilderness. In taking up his wilderness career, our sources mean to say, he turned his back upon the dwellings and the normal life of men, abandoning even the provision men make for a regular supply of food. Henceforth he dwelt where locusts and "wild honey" were the only edibles possibly available. How he survived under the circumstances was a mystery

13

which those inclined to think ill of him explained by the imputation of magic.

The second detail concerning John's life in the wilderness, namely, the camel's hair garment and the leather girdle, tradition has also seized upon, making them the garment of Elijah and the girdle of Elisha.[14] Modern commentators, while not insisting upon the identity of the articles themselves, have, nonetheless, continued to point to the fact that the hairy mantle is the mark of the Jewish prophet (Zech 13:4), and that the LXX version of 2 Kings 1:8 uses virtually the same words as Mark 1:6, when it describes Elijah as one who had "a leather girdle girded about his loins." That Mark and the other New Testament writers saw in the mantle and the girdle tokens of John's prophetic role and of his relation to Elijah is quite probable. For this they had other grounds and good and sufficient reason, but that John himself chose the garb in order to suggest prophetic authority and to conjure up allusions to Elijah is at least problematical. After all, the characteristic and most essential element of the nomad's dress in the Near East even today is still the *burnous* or flowing cloak that protects him against the burning sun by day and is wrapped close about him to shield him from the cold at night. In the Gospels the garments are said to be made from the hair of the camel, the very animal upon which the wilderness nomad has always depended for his sustenance, and in Old Testament days such garments probably became the typical garb of the prophet largely because the prophet was himself a man of the wilderness. Hence, it may well be that John's clothing was suggested not so much by his desire to symbolize Elijah, as by the elementary requirements of his wilderness sojourn.

How likely this is we learn from another word of Jesus about John. In Matthew 11:7–8 Jesus says to the crowds, "What went ye out into the wilderness to see? . . . A man dressed in soft garments? Behold they that wear soft garments are in kings' houses" (Mt 11:8 = Lk 7:25). Note that in this saying John's dress is interpreted as the diametrical opposite of "royal raiment." What this opposite was, an interesting passage in Josephus helps us to understand. In the passage in question (*Jewish War* I, 24, 3) the sons of Mariamne threaten to stage a protest against Herod's action in giving away their mother's court finery to his later wives. What they propose to do is to wear at court "garments made of hair" instead of their normal court attire. Now the impression the sons wish to create by their protest is naturally not that they are prophets, but that their father by giving away the treasures of the Maccabean house has reduced them to wilderness nomads, or, as we would say, to homeless paupers. Hence, their stage play. In clothing himself in a garment made of camel's hair, John, therefore, in all probability merely reduced himself also to the homespun of the nomad. Only what he did in the wilderness eventually suggested that his garb had a greater, prophetic significance.

Hitherto everything touched upon underlines the importance of the wilderness itself as a factor in the life of the Baptist. For John to live as he did and where he did, meant to separate himself from the normal, the safe-guarded, the planned life of men. Such separation implies a profound disregard of and simultaneously also a deep revulsion against the established cultural order. For this reason, it cannot be casual in origin, but must have its roots in some bitter experience that turned him perma-nently aside from the normal course of human life. Judg-ing by the violence of the reaction, the roots of John's alienation from the life of his day must lie very deep. Exactly what they were we can only conjecture, but a conjecture at least is in order. To develop it we must go back to the only evidence we have for the earlier phases of John's life, namely, the Infancy Narrative.

Significant for our understanding of the Baptist In-fancy Narrative is the work that has recently been done on the Lukan Nativity Story as a whole. The work has shown that Luke 1–2 is a combination of two series of parallel episodes held together by materials basically un-related to the thread of either series. Each series of epi-sodes—the one dealing with John, the other with Jesus— contains an act of annunciation, an account of birth, cir-cumcision and name-giving, an encomium in praise of the newly-born infant, and a concluding statement about the growth of the child.[15] Three conclusions are suggested by the analogy of the two series of episodes. The first is that the account of John's infancy (Lk 1:5–25 and 67–80) was originally—in an oral form—a complete, independent story. The second is that this Baptist Infancy Narrative may have had something to do with the development of the analogous story of Jesus' birth. The third is that the episode of Mary's visit to Elizabeth, the episode which Luke uses to knit the two parallel accounts together, is later than the rest of the material in point of origin. It is only the first of these conclusions with which we are concerned here.

When the story of John's birth is taken out of its larger setting and examined separately, its essentially Baptist character becomes thoroughly clear. The account shows not the slightest trace of the common Gospel tendency to subordinate John to Jesus and to regard him as Jesus' Forerunner. John's place in history is made quite plain by Gabriel's statement that he will "turn many of the children of Israel to the Lord their God," and will go before God himself "to turn the affections of the fathers to the children, to fill the disobedient with the wisdom of the just and to make ready for the Lord (God) a prepared people" (Lk 1:16–17). John is thus the one who will himself set the stage for the eschatological deliverance. As the herald of God's coming (Mal 3:1; 4:6; Sirach 48:10), he is properly endowed with the Spirit from his mother's womb and born in consequence of an act of divine intervention. When John has been born, Zacharias in the *Benedictus* can readily say that the day of redemption *has* come, and proclaim John as the one who will give the knowledge of salvation to God's people (Lk 1:68–79).

The autonomy and significance of John in the Infancy Narrative demands that the story arose in Baptist circles, and as an early Baptist narrative it requires careful consideration in any discussion of John's antecedents.

Closer scrutiny makes it perfectly evident that John's Infancy Narrative is a treasure-house of situations and motifs familiar from the Old Testament and from contemporary Jewish piety. Familiar to all readers of the Old Testament are accounts of angel visitation, such as that which came to Zacharias. Mysterious visitors seen and mysterious voices heard by priests officiating in the Temple are mentioned in the Talmud and by Josephus.[16] Zacharias and Elisabeth, the aged but childless couple to whom the birth of a child is divinely announced, have their counterpart in Abraham and Sarah (Gen 17–18), and in Manoah and his wife (Jud 13). Divine instructions concerning the name to be given a child reappear in the case of Ishmael (Gen 16:11), Isaac (Gen 17:19) and Solomon (1 Chron 22:9). Even the request for a sign giving assurance of the validity of a divine promise occurs repeatedly in the Old Testament (Gen 15:8; Jud 6:36; 2 Kgs 20:8). The difference between the answer to such requests in the Old Testament and the Infancy Narrative of John is that the generation to which the Baptist narrator belonged apparently doubted the propriety of the demand for a sign, and consequently chose to make the sign itself the punishment of the one who demanded it.[17]

The existence in Jewish religious literature and folk-

lore of analogies to virtually all the important elements
of John's birth story shows that the narrative is fundamentally legendary and that its episodes cannot be used
directly for historical purposes. What the story is trying
to do is to supply John with antecedents suited to the
unusual impression which he made upon people as God's
agent in the consummation of his purposes for his people.
It is the element of mystery attaching to John, the
preacher in the wilderness, that suggests his procreation
by divine intervention and his birth under unusual circumstances. We still catch the note of wonder suggested
by John's later life and projected back into his infancy
in the words of those who, having heard of his marvelous
birth, say, "What is to become of this child?" (Lk 1:66).
Only as a man about whom the faithful wondered, could
John be described in his birth and infancy as a wonderchild.

To recognize the legendary character of the Infancy
Narrative of John is to restrict its historical value, but
not necessarily to remove it entirely. It is important in
this connection to keep in mind the fundamental distinction between myth and legend, and to realize that
while myth creates for itself purely imaginary situations,
legend is only the imaginary embellishment of events or
processes in the historical order.[18] Whatever be true of
the incidence of legend, it is perfectly clear that there is
little if any myth in Gospel material. Both Christian and
Baptist thinking is much too conscious of its relation to
historical developments to encourage the growth of myth.

Dealing as we are, therefore, with legend, our problem is to find a way of abstracting from it its basic element of historical fact. The opportunity is provided here for testing the statement made in an earlier context that what men imagined and believed about such persons as John the Baptist is often as revealing as what they may be said to have known.

Now there is one particular in which the evidential character of the Baptist Infancy Narrative is beyond question, namely, as a record of the piety of the Baptist circles that created it. If we can set aside momentarily the question of what it tells us about events in the lives of John's parents, and inquire only about what it tells us of the people who created the story, we may yet be able to draw from it certain inferences concerning John's antecedents.

Clearly the circles that created the Baptist Infancy Narrative were deeply pious Jews. In its broad outlines their piety was traditional. It affirms the glorious record of the nation's history and upholds the hope of national deliverance. It exalts righteousness before God in the scrupulous observance of commandment and ordinance and reveals the confident assurance that God will reward the individual who is blameless before him. Consequently, it thrives on prayer to God for his blessings, including prayer for the gift of offspring, and finds in the answer to such prayer its own justification and triumph. It honors those who function by divine ordinance as the representatives of the people in the cult of the Temple.

In all these things the story reflects the piety of the common man in Israel, the man for whom the Psalter, so liberally quoted in the *Benedictus,* is the vehicle of religious self-expression.

In one particular only does the story depart from the point of view of the rank and file of Jews, namely, in the importance it attaches to the priest. In the birth story it is a priest, officiating in God's presence, to whom it is revealed that God's plan of national deliverance is about to be put into execution. The priest who has devoted himself to righteousness even though God has not blessed him outwardly, it implies, is able to understand that this plan of deliverance accomplishes above all the transformation of the sinner and the creation of a people prepared for the "dawn from on high." More than that, he can and does, himself, become an instrument of God for the achievement of his purpose and receives in that connection the reward of his own virtue.

The presence of this factor in the piety of the birth story is worthy of note and requires explanation. The important fact to keep in mind in this connection is that the circles with which the Jews of the period associated the coming of a national deliverance were normally those of the royal Davidic family, rather than the priestly clans. This fact is attested even in the Gospels, where, both by the genealogies and the Nativity Story, Jesus is connected with the house of David. The departure of the Baptist Infancy Narrative from this common standard is remarkable and cannot be the product of Christian influence. The only analogy to its point of view is that of the Book of Jubilees and of the original form of the Testament of the Twelve Patriarchs. In these products of the Maccabean uprising and monarchy, it is the priestly family of Levi that prepares the way for, or produces, the nation's deliverer.[19]

From what has been said, it seems necessary to infer that the circles which produced the Baptist birth story preserved some of the exalted conceptions of priestly destiny current in Judæa in the days when a family of priests, the Maccabeans, freed the nation from Seleucid oppression. The logical inference is that the Baptist movement in Judæa had a strong backhold in local priestly circles. Comparing our birth story and the earlier documents that express an analogous point of view, namely, the Book of Jubilees and the original form of the Testament of the Twelve Patriarchs, we find one significant difference between them. In the earlier works much of the emphasis falls upon the external, political aspects of the national deliverance, and the Maccabean family is, by implication at least, the chosen instrument for the consummation of God's purposes. In the Baptist birth story the deliverance has been spiritualized, for it is accomplished in connection with the remission to the people of their sins (Lk 1:77), and it is an otherwise obscure and outwardly unrewarded priest who serves as the father of God's chosen agent. If we take into account what is known about the secularization of the urban priesthood of Jerusalem and particularly of the Maccabean family in the period with which we are dealing, it seems clear that the landed, rural priesthood provides the best medium for the cultivation of the priestly ideals expressed in the Baptist birth story. The logical inference seems to be that the Baptist movement in Judæa had its backhold not merely in the priesthood but more particularly in rural priestly circles. How it came to have that backhold and produce this type of story would be especially intelligible if, as the story declares, John was himself the son of a rural priest. This conclusion, which can apparently be confirmed in other ways as we shall see, we are inclined actually to draw, and in this conclusion we find the historical nucleus of the Infancy Narrative of John.

What we have found it possible to infer about John's antecedents provides the starting point for a train of thought that is of fundamental importance for the interpretation of John's career and of vital significance for the answer to the question, what was it that drove John into the wilderness?

If John was, as seems likely, of priestly descent, he would, under normal circumstances, have followed in his father's footsteps and become a priest. This was not only a matter of a professional option open to him, but a sacred obligation imposed upon him by the choice God had made among the descendants of the sons of Jacob as to which should minister before him at the altar. For John not to fulfill this sacred obligation is in itself quite as strange as for him to turn his back upon the settled life of men and to dwell henceforth in the wilderness. It is a fair hypothesis that these two strange aspects of his career are interrelated. For their interrelation it is possible, with a knowledge of contemporary affairs in the Jewish priesthood, to develop a set of favorable circumstances.

Random statements in Josephus and the Talmud reveal that in the first century of our era a sharp cleavage was developing in the Jewish priesthood between the urban aristocracy of Jerusalem and their less pretentious landed colleagues who lived most of the year in the towns and hamlets of Judæa and came to the Temple but two weeks in each year when it was the turn of their particular class to participate in the performance of the sacrifices. Three factors played an important part in these developments. The first and least important for our purposes is the tendency of both the Herods and the Roman procurators to appoint and depose high priests at will, making the office a pawn in the game of national politics. Josephus lists no less than twenty-eight high priests in the century preceding the fall of Jerusalem. The second is the tendency of certain of the families from among whose members the high priests were chosen to act in ways ill becoming their station. Significant in this connection are the "woes" uttered by a rabbi of the early second century over the high-priestly families of the Herodian and procuratorial period of Jewish history. The "woes" reported in the tractate Pesachim of the *Babylonian Talmud* read as follows:

Woe is me because of the house of Boethus; woe is
me because of their staves;

Woe is me because of the house of Hanin; woe is
me because of their whisperings.

Woe is me because of the house of Kathros; woe
is me because of their pens.

Woe is me because of the house of Ishmael the son
of Phabi; woe is me because of their fists.

For they are high priests and their sons are (Temple) treasurers, and their sons-in-law are
trustees and their servants beat the people
with staves.[20]

Abba Hanin, the author of these "woes," may be exaggerating as he looks back upon the past, but his diatribe
is scarcely without some foundation in fact. That foundation in fact would seem to be the appearance of arrogance,
of nepotism in the distribution of administrative office,
and of the growth of bureaucratic tendencies among the
important priestly families resident in Jerusalem. The
third factor in the historical situation is the habit of the
higher priestly circles to appropriate, by violence if need
be, more than their share of the priestly perquisites.
Josephus tells of poorer priests actually dying of hunger
in the days just prior to the outbreak of the Jewish War
because the high priests seized the tithes upon which
they depended for their sustenance. The Talmud mentions disputes over the division of perquisites at an earlier
time.[21] In a measure the urban priests were no doubt

justified in demanding a larger proportion of the contributions which the pious made to the upkeep of the priesthood, for they had no backhold in agricultural enterprise as the rural priests had, and their urban establishments were far more expensive to maintain. Yet their tendency to appropriate for themselves increasing sums had the effect of reducing the lower ranks to the level of peasantry, thereby accentuating the distinction between the two groups.

If John as a youth in his twenties followed the normal procedure and applied at Jerusalem for ordination to holy office, he may have realized here for the first time, if he came of rural priestly parents, the disadvantages accruing to him on that score. As one brought up in a modest environment, he may well have been quite unable to cope with life on the complicated and magnificent scale in which it was lived by the more secularized priestly officialdom of Jerusalem. For the urbanized officials of the priesthood he may have been just another rustic come to claim his share of the perquisites, and, for such of their sons as were his fellows in candidacy for ordination, someone to be brushed aside in their own progress toward a brilliant career. If John brought with him such ideals of the sanctity and significance of the priesthood as come to expression in the Infancy Narrative and are focused there in the venerable figure of his own father, he may well have been led to regard what he saw going on at Jerusalem as a desecration of a high calling, jeopardizing the nation's acceptability before God and destined only to bring the wrath of a jealous God down upon his faith-less servants. The analogy here is to Jesus' own experience at the fatal Passover, when the spectacle of the Holy City preparing to celebrate the Feast of the National Deliverance without heeding his call to repentance and to national consecration provoked his most violent acts, elicited his direst prophecies and gave to his words the note of pathos and sadness. Allowing for John's more vindictive temperament, the situation confronting him could well have led him to turn his back upon the priestly calling with a profound sense of revulsion against its representatives. For John to have taken such a step could well have rendered him quite unintelligible to the simpler folk of his native environment, with their deep reverence for the priestly office, making life equally in-tolerable for him there and sending him forth in bitter anguish of soul into the wilderness.

All this is hypothesis, a twentieth-century "legend" that endeavors to account for an important historical fact from the materials available. Yet whatever be true about this particular suggestion, it is clear that without a catastrophic experience of some sort, John would scarcely have become a dweller in the wilderness.

It would be a mistake, however, to conclude from what has been said, that the function of the wilderness sojourn in John's career was entirely negative, and that it served merely as the means of separation from some-thing or as protest against something. The wilderness was to the ancient more than a place devoid of human habitation and remote from man-made civilization. It was, at the same time, the place where man came most immediately into contact with supernatural powers. The wilderness has apparently always had such connotations in the mind of the Oriental. We catch glimpses of this in primitive Semitic religious belief, in the tales of the Christian anchorites and in later Arabic folklore. Yet the book that would gather all the material together and bring into focus the importance of the desert for the development of ancient oriental religious thought has yet to be written.

It is not necessary to go far afield in order to show what the associations of the wilderness were to the Jews of ancient Palestine. The material is close at hand in the familiar literature of the Biblical period. On the one hand, sojourn in the wilderness meant exposure to dangers —dangers of wild beasts, and more particularly of evil demonic powers. We find evidence of this from the earlier period in the wilderness demon Azazel to whom the scapegoat of the atonement ritual is given over (Lev 16:8–10) and in the demonic seducers of IV Maccabees 18:8, who haunt the empty places. In the New Testament it is the Parable of the Demon and the Empty Heart (Mt 12:43), Luke's embellishment of the story of the Gerasene Demoniac (Lk 8:29), and, above all, the Temptation Story that provide the relevant material.[22] Mark's version of the Temptation Story (1:13) is particularly significant in this connection. It has the temptation procedure cover the entire forty days of Jesus' wilderness sojourn, locates

28

the whole experience in the wilderness and surrounds Jesus there with both the forces of evil and the wild beasts. To the ancient who read the brief account the picture was complete without the enumeration of specific episodes such as the Second Source, in its more intellectualized version, tried to offer. To live in the wilderness forty days was indeed to be exposed continually to tremendous dangers — natural and supernatural — and for Mark to indicate that in the midst of these dangers the heavenly angels ministered to Jesus was enough to reassure the reader that God was guiding the destinies of his Son. For John to take up his abode in the wilderness was to risk exposure to these same dangers, and because there were demons there it could be said he had a demon at his beck and call.

But the association of the wilderness with the supernatural is not limited to the category of the demonic and the Satanic. In the wilderness the ancient Hebrew found God and his angels. It was in the wilderness of Sinai that Moses found Yahweh. It was under the juniper tree in the wilderness that Elijah encountered the Angel of the Lord (1 Kgs 19:4–8). It was the herdsman of the wilderness of Tekoa, Amos, who became the inspiration for the greatest period in the history of early Hebrew prophecy. Between the prophet and the wilderness a relation seems to exist that makes the dress of the wilderness dweller the characteristic garb of the prophet (Zech 13:4), as we have already seen, and that makes the only correct answer to Jesus' question, "What went ye out into the wilderness to see?", the answer which he himself gives, "To see a prophet? Yes, I tell you even more than a prophet" (Mt 11:9).

John was not by any means the only one who, in first century Palestine, reveals the association of those claiming special endowment by God with the wilderness environment. Josephus has a number of stories to tell about men who tried to lead the people astray in the last decades of the history of the Second Temple, men whom he calls "deceivers" but who seem to claim for themselves messianic or prophetic endowment. These deceivers, so-called, frequently begin by urging the people to follow them into the wilderness to receive there the proof of the claims put forth.[23] The same phenomenon apparently played a part in the life of the early Palestinian Church, for Matthew explicitly warns the faithful that if anyone comes saying of the returned Christ, "Lo, he is in the wilderness," they are not to believe it (Mt 24:26).

What creates the relation between the prophet and the wilderness is not so much the prophet's desire for seclusion or even his protest against the foibles of the day, but rather, it would seem, the clarification of insight and understanding that comes to him there and that he associates with the influence of the divine presence. Gospel story is insistent in the connection it makes between Jesus' search for guidance in prayer and meditation and the "solitary places," that is, the wilderness in an adjectival use of the term. The wilderness must have had something of the same meaning also for the Baptist,

30

because in the wilderness John became what he had not
been before—a preacher, a man who felt himself divinely
inspired to speak to his people, first, no doubt, to such
travelers as passed him at the crossroads, then to the
ever-growing company of those who sought him out.

The analogy to Biblical prophecy suggests that the
change which came over John in the wilderness, transforming him from a disillusioned neophyte priest to a
"shining light," did not occur without some crucial religious experience that both clarified his thought and
gave him the sense of authority to speak on behalf of
God. To this experience there is but a single allusion in
the New Testament, namely, in Luke 3:1–2, where we
are told that the "word of God came to John in the
wilderness," this being in the fifteenth year of the reign
of the Emperor Tiberius. The statement, though prob-
lematic, is highly important in providing the only valid
suggestion of a specific date for the beginning of John's
public career, namely, in all probability the year 27–28
A.D.[24] Yet it is disappointing as the record of a *Beru-
fungsvision*. Clearly there must have existed in oral Baptist tradition, even in New Testament times, an explicit
narrative of how the "call" came to John, but the Evangelists have chosen not to perpetuate it for reasons best
known to themselves.

What the "crowds" heard from the inspired lips in
the wilderness conjured up in their minds reminiscences
of the greatest among the spokesmen of God as they
knew them from Biblical narrative. What John pro-

31

claimed, in strict conformity to his revulsion against the existing order, was a message of impending doom and disaster. This portentous proclamation, delivered in words whose feverish heat reflects the intensity of the fires of his inspiration, is necessarily our next concern.

II

John's Preaching: The Proclamation

THAT John proclaimed in no uncertain terms a message of crucial significance for his people is an essential part of the tradition about his life and work. The importance of what he said is heavily underscored by the words "preached," "cried" and "witnessed" with which many of his utterances are introduced in the Gospels, and also by the general remarks about the impression that he made, to wit, the statement of Mark that "all the country of Judæa and all the people of Jerusalem went out to him" (Mk 1:5), and the statement of Josephus that the people "seemed likely to do everything he might counsel."[1]

Of the content of John's preaching we have only a limited knowledge. Later Baptist legend, lacking both the native intelligence and the moral fervor to cope with the topic, scarcely broaches it at all.[2] Among the earlier sources, even Josephus is of no help, for in trying to adapt his work to the taste of Roman readers he has watered down John's message till it becomes no more than an encomium of virtue with the purification of the body by baptism thrown in for good measure. It is hard to see how such a message could have given John enough of a hold upon the people to make Herod fear an insurrection, as Josephus says he did. For our knowledge of John's preaching we are, therefore, thrown back again upon the New Testament documents.

The New Testament contains two types of information bearing upon the subject: first, general statements describing the message, such as Mark's affirmation that John came "preaching a baptism of repentance for the remission of sins" (Mk 1:4), which Matthew has expanded to include a reference to the imminence of the Kingdom (Mt 3:2); and second, specific words of the Baptist quoted directly as such. Of the two types the latter is naturally the more important for our purposes and must form the starting point of our analysis, but even here certain allowances have to be made. Among the canonical Evangelists, the fourth is unfortunately not as reliable as the other three in his rendering of the specific utterances, for he telescopes them, adapts them to the purposes of his advanced pre-existence Christology, and in general uses them to make John the first confessing Christian.[3] In contrast, the Synoptic forms of the sayings are in general trustworthy. Those least well attested are intrinsically the least open to objection, and those that might be most readily suspected can be observed and controlled over the longest period of time as they are transmitted from one document to another.[4] Such modification as occurs in the course of this transmission is slight and can usually be identified as the result of random attempts to graft a Christian meaning upon a non-Christian stock by the simplest of devices.

Altogether we have only ten specific sayings of John from which to reconstruct the content and nature of his preaching. Nine of them come up through the oral tradition into the written record in blocks of three without narrative setting. One block is doubly attested by Mark and the Second Source, one comes only from the Second Source, and one is preserved in Luke alone. Set down in their simplest form according to the blocks and sources in which they appear, the nine words are as follows:

Block A (Mark and the Second Source), Mark 1:7–8; Matthew 3:11–12 = Luke 3:16–17.

1. After me there comes one who is mightier than I, the thong of whose sandal I am unworthy to stoop down and loosen.

2. I baptize you with water, but he will baptize you with Holy Spirit (or: with Holy Spirit and with fire).

3. His fan is in his hand and he will cleanse his threshing floor and gather his grain together in the granary, but the chaff he will burn with un-

quenchable fire. (This is not in Mark but belongs apparently to the same block.)

Block B (from the Second Source), Matthew 3:7–10 = Luke 3:7–9.

4. Brood of vipers, who has showed you that you will escape the coming wrath.

5. Produce fruits worthy of repentance, and do not think to say, "We have Abraham for our father," for I tell you God can raise up children to Abraham from these stones.

6. Already the axe lies at the root of the trees. Every tree, therefore, that does not bring forth good fruit will be cut down and thrown into the fire.

Block C (from Luke only), Luke 3:10–14.

7. The crowds asked him saying, "What are we to do?" But he answered saying to them, "Whoever has two shirts, let him share with him who has none, and whoever has food, let him do likewise."

8. The tax-collectors came to be baptized and said to him, "What are we to do?" But he said to them, "Exact no more than the established tax rate allows."

9. Even the soldiers asked him saying, "And what are we to do?" And he said to them, "Do not apply violence for personal gain; do not lay false charges; and be satisfied with your wages."

To these nine words we must add as the tenth, the one preserved by Mark (6:18) in a narrative context, namely, the word addressed to Herod Antipas,

10. It is not lawful for thee to have thy brother's wife.

All these sayings have one thing in common. They represent not counsels of wisdom but rather the pronouncements of one who feels himself authorized to be a spokesman of God. They have about them the ring of authority. What they utter is threat, promise and command. This means that they fall into the traditional categories of prophetic speech as we know it from the Old Testament. With the pronouncements of the earlier days they share the vividness that comes from the use of metaphor (the winnowing fan, the threshing floor, the axe and the trees, the brood of vipers) and from the use of paradox (children from stones, baptism with Spirit). If they are rendered in prose rather than in the poetic form of so much of Israel's earlier prophecy, they do not by that token descend to the remoteness or copy the wild imaginings of contemporary apocalyptic writers. Their prose serves only to make them more direct and more brutally frank in character. That in words such as these many found the voice of prophecy reborn and bowed before its authority is readily intelligible.

Classified as to function and character the ten sayings fall into three groups. One group of four, comprising the words to the crowds, the tax-collectors and the sol-

diers and the general instruction, "Produce fruits worthy
of repentance," is hortatory in character, giving ethical
injunctions. A second group of four, comprising the words
about the axe and the trees, the fan and the threshing
floor, the mightier one and the second baptism, is kergy-
matic in character, giving expression to a divine proclamation. The third group of two, namely, the word "It
is not lawful" and the word about the brood of vipers,
is denunciatory in character. For our purposes it will be
well to associate John's denunciation of Herod with the
hortatory group and his word about the brood of vipers
with the kerygmatic group, reducing the three groups to
two and thus providing the division between this and the
following chapters, which deal with John's proclamation
and John's exhortation respectively.

Of John's kerygmatic sayings the words about the
threshing floor, the trees of the orchard and the brood of
vipers bear directly upon one and the same theme. It is
the familiar yet always terrible theme of the divine judgment. There is scarcely a prophet in the many centuries
from Amos on in whose proclamation it failed to find
expression. Basic to the importance of the theme in the
thought of Israel's prophets is the grandiose conception
that the broad sweep and the tremendous convulsions of
history are under the control of the one Almighty God.
That God's control of the historical process involved acts
of judgment was suggested by two things. The first was
God's covenant with Israel, from which it followed that
all threats to his people's security and autonomy must

bring his retributive punishment upon the nation's oppressors. The second was the ethical character of God's power and will. From this it followed that when Israel itself fell short of righteousness before God, it too must feel the sting of his chastisement. The history of prophecy in Israel is the record of a succession of men who, in days of internal and external crisis, proclaimed the imminence of such divine retribution upon the nations and the Chosen People. Many times the proclamation had been uttered and more than once it had been validated to some extent by subsequent developments, but never in that final and definitive way that the thought of God's absolute and unqualified sovereignty suggested. Meanwhile, in the minds of some at least, doubts had arisen whether by individual acts of judgment within the historical process, the divine sovereignty could ever come to full and final expression. So the issue hung in the balance, and the question is what had John to add to the picture.

The words about the threshing floor and the trees of the orchard paint in a few bold strokes pictures of the agricultural life of Palestine, pictures that have a long history in the metaphorical language of Hebrew prophecy. The figure of the threshing floor recalls at once the Servant Lyric of Second Isaiah, in which God says to Israel:

I will make thee to be a threshing-sledge,
Yea, a new sledge armed with teeth;
Thou shalt thresh mountains and shatter them,

Hills thou shalt make as chaff.
Thou shalt winnow and the wind shall scatter them,
They shall be scattered by the tempest;
But thou shalt exult in Yahweh,
In the Holy One of Israel shalt thou glory.
    (Is 41:15–16)

The passage is important because it develops the figure in all its vivid details. Not every user of the metaphor had occasion to be so explicit, but the basic comparison and its several elements appear separately in many other parts of the Old Testament. Amos describes the atrocities which Damascus committed against Israel by saying that it threshed Gilead with threshing instruments of iron (Amos 1:3). Jeremiah compares Babylon in its impending downfall to the threshing floor that is leveled off and stamped down, and in the same breath, also, to the grain that is threshed upon its surface (Jer 51:33). Habakkuk calls God's judgment a threshing of the nations (3:12), and in Micah, God summons Israel to thresh the nations whom he has gathered as sheaves on the threshing floor (4:13). From the repeated use of the metaphor there develops the standard comparison of the wicked with the "chaff which the wind bloweth away," a comparison that we find in all parts of the Old Testament.[5]

While in earlier prophecy the judgment described by the figure is usually an historical episode in which a single nation acts as God's instrument to punish other nations,

in the later period the import of the figure grows. A good
example of the later usage is to be found in IV Ezra,
where an interpreting angel explains to Salathiel the
abundance of human misfortune by saying:

> A grain of evil seed was sown in the heart of Adam
> from the beginning, and how much fruit has it pro-
> duced to this time and shall yet produce till the
> threshing floor come. (4:30)

Here the threshing floor is God's judgment not upon the
nations but upon man and his unrighteous acts. How
inclusive this judgment is we can gather from the immediate context, where Salathiel, bemoaning the continued subjection of his people to the godless nations
and the unhappy intermediate state of the departed souls,
finally is led to conclude:

> Behold we are all full of unrighteousness. Is it per-
> chance on our account that the threshing floor of
> the departed righteous is held back—on account of
> the sins of the dwellers on the earth? (4:38–39)

Here the threshing floor is a metaphor for a universal,
final judgment in which even the dead will participate.
To give Israel a chance to repent the coming of the judgment has been held back. Yet it will surely come when
the number of the saints has been completed.[6]
  John's use of the metaphor presupposes these developments. We gather this from the fact that in his word

about the threshing floor the chaff is to be burned in "unquenchable fire." Unquenchable fire is certainly not the natural medium for the removal of a heap of chaff. The fact that the fire is unquenchable shows that the metaphor of the threshing floor is breaking down in John's hands under the impact of ideas too momentous to be expressed by it. Judgment has become a cosmic event of such scope and magnitude that it beggars analogy in terms of human experience.

John's word about the trees with the axe at their roots also has its background in the Old Testament. In a country where even in antiquity trees were not too plentiful they were naturally subject to close scrutiny and to frequent comment. We Westerners, whom nature has supplied with a more diversified climate and a richer measure of the fruits of nature, find it hard to realize that trees and springs, animals and flowers and even clouds can have for the Oriental associations belonging to the realm of the numinous. It takes a sojourn in the Orient to make one understand the element of wonder that attaches to the appearance of the first cloud after months of brazen skies, the miracle of vegetation reborn after the rains where for months nothing but rock and dust has been visible, and the profound mystery of the tree that grows no one knows how and of the spring that draws its supply of precious water no one knows whence. It is not strange under the circumstances that Israel's neighbors found in the tree the symbol and the living manifestation of a nature deity.[7] Israel itself was more circumspect in this particular, for its God was not a nature god but a creator god. Consequently, the Hebrew writers see in the tree, its growth from tender seedling to vigorous maturity, its aging and its eventual fall, a symbol of the next most significant factor on the cosmic scene, the human being and the nation. In this sense we find the tree a common metaphor of many Old Testament documents.

Of the many passages that reflect the comparison the most familiar is, of course, that of Psalm 1:3,

> He shall be like a tree planted by the streams of
>   water,
> That bringeth forth its fruit in due season,
> Whose leaf also does not wither.

Equally familiar is Jotham's parable (Jud 9) in which the trees' search for a king is the counterpart of the nation's search for a monarch. Prophecy in the earlier and in the later post-canonical period regularly uses the figure, whether speaking of the individual Israelite (Jer 17:8), of the Chosen People (Is 61:3) and its several elements (Jer 11:16, 19; Ezek 15:6), of foreign rulers (Ezek 31:1–18) or foreign nations (Amos 2:9; Is 10:15–19; Dan 4), or of all the nations of mankind (IV Ezra 9:20–22; II Baruch 36).

Prophets speak of trees particularly in metaphors of judgment, comparing the fate of the wicked to that of trees that wither or are uprooted or cut down or destroyed by fire, God himself acting as woodcutter. An interesting example of the usage is the passage in Isaiah 10:33–34:

> Behold the Lord, Yahweh of Hosts, will lop the boughs with terror, and the high of stature will be hewn down and the lofty shall be brought low. And he will cut down the thickets of the forest with iron, and Lebanon shall fall by the mighty one.

Here in the words of the pre-exilic prophet we are already close to the spirit and the application of John's use of the figure. Yet there are two characteristic differences. Prophetic usage makes the trees of the forest the symbol of the nations, and those of the orchard a symbol of the People of Israel. Hence, when they allude to the cutting of trees in a figure of judgment, the prophets always specify the trees of the forest, that is, the Gentiles, never the fruit trees, that is, Israel. The only exceptions to this rule are in the Wisdom Literature.[8] In John's saying, it is the trees of the orchard that are to be hewn down if they do not bring forth good fruit. It is God's own planting, it is Israel itself upon which the judgment impends, and this judgment, the second characteristic difference tells us, will be drastic indeed. For, instead of being saved and used for domestic and manufacturing purposes, as would normally be the case in as poor a country as Palestine, the wood will be consumed in a flaming holocaust till nothing remains but a heap of ashes.

By his use of the threshing floor and the tree metaphor John, therefore, places himself squarely in the prophetic tradition. With the prophets of old he declares that the history of men and of nations has movement and direction. Like trees and crops, men individually and collectively have their periods of infancy, growth and maturity. But the fact of growth and development is not to be regarded as self-evident. The mysterious power of growth that the tree has is divinely given for a specific purpose, and if the tree of the orchard does not produce the fruit it is intended to provide, that is more than merely unfortunate. The tree has lost its fundamental right to existence in God's purposeful order, and its removal is a necessary element of that order. So it is with men and with nations. They, too, have mysterious powers of growth and development, but these are not prerogatives, they are the media for the fulfillment of a divine purpose. It is God who gives meaning to history, not men and nations, and because God does so, history must have a terrible end for him who fails to play his part in its appointed course. So for John, as for the prophets before him, the thought of the final judgment has its roots in a profound conception of history from which it derives its ultimate compulsions. Since Israel stands in the center of that historical process, it faces in a special sense the threat of that judgment.

That the saying introduced by the denunciatory epithet "brood of vipers" also bears upon the subject of the final judgment, requires no demonstration. The "coming wrath" which it announces is a familiar theme of Hebrew thought and literature. From the very earliest days of Israel's history the passionate nature of its God Yahweh was thoroughly understood. Thus, his nature manifested itself, on the one hand, in an intense jealousy toward other gods, and, on the other, in the anger and the vengefulness which he exhibited toward those who acted in disobedience of their covenant with him. The prophets since Amos discovered in Yahweh's moral character an ethical basis for his wrath, and, as the expression of his bitter enmity toward sin, they did not cease to proclaim it. All of the misfortunes and disasters of individual and national life were regarded as the result of its operation, and when the concept of a great final judgment, universal in scope and absolute in significance developed, it could be and was regarded as the supreme manifestation of God's anger, and came to be known as the "day of wrath" (e.g. Jubilees 24:28, 30, 36:10; Rom 2:5). In picking up this theme John shows clearly what terrors were associated in his mind with the coming event.

More important for our immediate purposes is the question to whom John was addressing himself when he uttered these words. Interpreters differ at this point, as well they may, for two alternatives are offered by our sources. The first alternative is that John was speaking to the Jews as a people. This is ultimately the suggestion of Luke, who mentions "the multitude" that came to be baptized (3:7), and seems to be supported by the saying that follows, in which reliance upon Abrahamic descent is discouraged. The second alternative is that John was speaking only to certain elements of the Jewish people.

This is ultimately the suggestion of Matthew, who specifies the Pharisees and the Sadducees as the persons addressed (3:7). Modern commentators, aware of Matthew's tendency to introduce references to his pet aversion at the slightest provocation, have substituted for the Pharisees and Sadducees those coming to baptism with improper motives, that is, those using it without a true sense of repentance.[9]

It is important to note, in this connection, that the word of John is reported twice in Gospel record as a saying of Jesus, once in Matthew 23:33, where Jesus says:

> "Snakes, brood of vipers, how will you escape the judgment of Gehenna?"

and again in a somewhat modified form in Matthew 12:34, where Jesus says:

> "Brood of vipers, how can you speak that which is good, being yourselves evil."

That the word of the Baptist has here become a saying of Jesus is significant for our knowledge of the early relations between Christian and Baptist circles as we shall see in another context. What matters in the present context is the inference that, to have been so readily transferred, the saying must at first have been current separately, in isolation from other words of the Baptist. This means that the setting in which Matthew and Luke bring it as a word of the Baptist cannot be considered normative for its interpretation. We are thrown back, therefore, on the word itself, and find in it two direct clues to its original application. The first is the introductory epithet, "brood of vipers." A distinction has to be made here between the connotation of the snake (the *ophis*) and the viper (the *echidna*). The snake had for the oriental the associations of craftiness, deceit and trickery, being, as the story of the Fall relates, the most subtile of the beasts of the field. The viper, on the other hand, was basically noxious in character, a creature of venomous malignity.[10] To call someone a "viper" is, therefore, not merely to accuse him of improper motives, but to castigate him as evil in his innermost being. What John is saying here is what Paul said when, according to Acts, he called Elymas a "son of the devil" and "the enemy of all righteousness."

The second clue to the meaning of the word about the "brood of vipers" is contained in the query, "Who has showed you that you will escape the coming wrath?" The word "show" contained in this query is invariably associated in New Testament usage with subjects that are not intelligible by themselves or in terms of common sense, but require special insight or instruction, particularly in the will of God.[11] In the present context the insight is of course imagined, for the persons are essentially wicked. But the allusion to the supposed insight coupled with the epithet "vipers" serves to make the saying bitterly ironical. We might, therefore, paraphrase the statement as follows: You children of Satan, whose heart is evil within you, on the strength of your imagined insight into the will of God you believe that you will escape the wrath of God's judgment day. What perverted minds you have! The source of your mistaken belief is not God but Satan himself. If God has singled you out for anything, it is not the receipt of his self-revelation but rather the experience of his righteous anger. Surely destruction in Gehenna will be your lot.

Interpreted in this way the saying about the "brood of vipers" is far too bitter to be addressed to the nation as a whole in which John found many who took repentance seriously and probably, also, too specific in its allusions to refer to those coming to baptism with improper motives. We are dealing, instead, with a special group that claims for itself prerogatives based upon assumed understanding of the divine will. Such a sense of prerogative would be particularly intelligible if the group in question felt itself constituted by divine ordinance. Of all the various groups in the Judaism of John's day, it is the priestly aristocracy that comes closest to fulfilling these requirements. Here was a group conscious of its prerogatives as the divinely instituted medium for the reconciliation of God and man, but one which at the same time tended to substitute arrogance for the essential virtues of righteousness and integrity in its relation to others and in the performance of its vocation. This group John could know intimately, and from his familiarity with its presumption gain the inspiration for the sharpest and most contemptuous saying that men recalled his having uttered. If it was the priesthood of which John was speaking when he denounced the "brood of vipers," he was only repeating in more colorful language what Malachi had said in the words:

> And now, O ye priests, this commandment is for you. If ye will not hear, and if ye lay it not to heart to give glory to my name, saith Yahweh of Hosts, then I will send a curse upon you, and I will curse your blessings (Mal 2:1–2).

It was a final universal judgment, then, a judgment beginning with the house of Israel and bringing retribution above all to its priests that John proclaimed in the wilderness. And that judgment, so all three of the words we have studied tell us, is destined to begin now, in the present. The wrath of God is on the march; the axe lies at the foot of the tree; the thresher has the threshing fan in his hand; history has reached its appointed end; every man's eternal destiny hangs in the balance and woe to those whom the divine wrath overtakes.

How this thought of the imminence of judgment could have arisen in John's mind, or in that of any other similarly minded person, and how it could become sufficiently powerful as a conviction to be made the basis of an inspired proclamation, we cannot know. We stand, at this point, face to face with the essential mystery of prophetic insight and divine inspiration. Among the factors which may have contributed to its crystallization the most significant is undoubtedly a vivid sense of the power and majesty of God himself. Given such a sense of God's majesty, rooted in his pious upbringing and intensified by his sojourn in the wilderness, it necessarily followed for John that the God of history must bring to realization the purposes which history was intended to serve. Indeed, the more profound the sense of God's power, the greater the tendency to foreshorten the perspective upon the time of that realization. But something more than this was needed—a hurt, a wound in those areas of the mind where the highest ideals and the ultimate values of the self and of the national life are enshrined, an injury so painful and serious that it could become symbolic of a Satanic threat to God's pre-eminence. To such a hurt so universalized, the proclamation of an imminent judgment would be a fitting reaction. If the hurt was caused by an experience involving the Jerusalem priesthood, it is natural that John should have uttered over the priests the direst threats of the divine wrath.

That the imminence of judgment was the basic element of John's proclamation cannot be doubted. The question is whether there was a second element in the proclamation, namely, a declaration concerning the coming of a Messiah, and if so, how the Messiah and the judgment are related in John's message. On this point our later sources are distinctly at odds. Josephus gives no inkling of any messianic factor in John's preaching, and what is more important, the addition of such a factor would change beyond recognition the idyllic picture of the Baptist as a humble teacher of righteousness that

Josephus constructs. By contrast, the Fourth Evangelist regards John as the classic Witness of the Messiah; that is, as a man whose every word and act testifies directly to the imminent fulfillment of the messianic hope in the person of the incarnate Word. That the account of the Fourth Gospel is untrustworthy in this particular we have already seen. But Josephus' silence is also suspect, for he is known to gloss over or suppress aspects of his people's life and thought that might weaken their case before the forum of Roman public opinion.[12] Because of their political implications, messianic hopes are never mentioned in his works, though certain of the persons whom he describes as brigands and deceivers must really have been messianic pretenders. With the later sources canceling each other out, we turn again to the Synoptic Gospels, but even here the evidence is not completely concordant.

That all three Synoptic Evangelists understood John's proclamation to involve a messianic element is perfectly obvious, otherwise they would not have given him a place in their Gospels as the Forerunner of the Messiah Jesus. On the other hand, in the Infancy Narrative, at least Luke preserves old Baptist materials which might seem to reflect an opposite point of view. Typical of this material is the inspired utterance of Zacharias about the infant John, namely:

And thou, child, shalt be called
The prophet of the Most High,

THE PROCLAMATION

For thou shalt go before the face of the Lord
   To make ready his ways,
To give knowledge of salvation unto his people
   In the remission of their sins
By the tender mercy of our God
With which the dayspring from on high shall visit us.
   (Lk 1:76–78)

As early as Mark's day the Christians interpreted the "Lord" whose way John was to prepare as none other than the Lord Jesus Christ. But this is not necessarily John's own position, for in the prophecy of Malachi, from which the words are taken, the Lord whom the messenger precedes is clearly God himself. Since the coming of a Messiah was not an inevitable part of the eschatological expectation of his day, John may, like Malachi, have lacked the messianic factor in his proclamation, or, if he included it, it may have been somewhat different from that which the Evangelists imputed to him. Which of these alternatives is correct depends ultimately upon the interpretation of John's utterances about the Mightier One and about the two baptisms. With these two Baptist sayings we have, therefore, to concern ourselves.

The word about the Mightier One who comes after John and whose sandals John is not fit to loose, appears in the New Testament in no less than seven forms (Mk 1:17; Mt 3:11; Lk 3:16; Acts 13:25; Jn 1:27, 15, 30), each slightly different from the others. Most of the dif-

53

ferences in the subordinate clause about the sandals can readily be accounted for as variations from a primitive form that reads: "the thong of whose sandals I am not fit to loose."[13] The variants in the main clause derive ultimately from two different formulations of it, namely:

1. There comes after me one who is mightier than I,
2. The one who comes after me is mightier than I.[14]

The first of these (There comes after me) is a proclamation about the coming of a Mightier One. The second (The one who comes after me) is a confession about the might of the one who is to come after John. In a Christian context the confessional form has to be discounted. Hence the basic form of the word is probably, "There comes after me one who is mightier than I, the thong of whose sandals I am not fit to loose."

In its main outlines the meaning of this form of the saying is quite clear. It is a pronouncement about one who can be and is being compared to John, albeit to the latter's disadvantage. The fact of the comparison shows that the person in question is not God, for to compare oneself with God, even in the most abject humility, would have been presumptuous for any Jew in John's day. The chances are, therefore, that the saying proclaims the coming of a Messiah, but whether as a messianic proclamation it reflects John's own preaching depends upon the kind of Messiah suggested. For the identification of the expected Messiah, the reference to the act of loosening the sandal thong is not of decisive importance, for it belongs to the realm of metaphor and cannot be pressed. Recent interpreters are, therefore, right in regarding the expressions "there comes after me" and "one mightier than I" as decisive for the sense and genuineness of the utterance.

It has been observed lately that the expression "to come after someone" or "to follow after someone" is frequently used in the New Testament to describe the relation of disciples to their master, as when Jesus says, "If anyone would come after me, let him deny himself" (Mk 6:34). Starting from this observation, John's utterance has been interpreted as a paradox in which he intimates that the Mightier One is one of his own disciples, while at the same time he, the master, is not worthy to be the disciple's slave.[15] If this interpretation is correct, the saying is in all probability a Christian invention, for it reflects too accurately the relation between Jesus and John as the Evangelists understand it. But the verb "to come" in eschatological contexts has other connotations than those of discipleship, and since the birth story speaks of John as "going before," it seems much more natural to keep the traditional association between "going before" and "coming after" than to inject the discipleship factor into the saying for which, after all, the expression "follow after" would be more appropriate.[16] This means, however, that we cannot determine the meaning and the genuineness of the saying from its verbs and throws us back upon the emigmatic words, "one mightier than I."

These words, too, have recently received comment,

the suggestion being that they should be interpreted in the light of Jesus' saying:

> When a mighty one, clad in armor, guards his court his possessions are undisturbed. But when the one mightier than he comes and conquers him, he seizes the armament upon which he relied and distributes his spoil. (Lk 11:21–22)

In the language of this saying, it is said, we have the most primitive of all christological terminology. Satan guarding his court is the Mighty One, and the Messiah who comes and conquers him is by contrast the Mightier One. Similarly, when John spoke of One Mightier he was referring to the Messiah and that in his capacity as the one to rout the forces of Satan.[17] So interpreted, the saying of John could well be genuine, but the difficulty is that the interpretation allegorizes a parable of Jesus and that the comparison is not between Satan and the Mightier, but between John and the Mightier, where the allusion to the rout of Satan is quite out of place. Actually of course, the classic associations of the verbs "to be strong" and to "have power" are all in the sphere of deity, and when, in a religious context, a person is said to "be mighty" or "mightier" this normally describes him as an agent of God. The only real question is what particular purpose the delegation by God of his power may be said to serve. The answer to this question, I believe, is contained in the comparison of John and the Mightier One. John himself has power, or "is mighty" because God has empowered him to proclaim judgment. If the one who comes after him is "mightier," then because of the analogy between them the Mightier One must execute the judgment which John proclaims. The Mightier One is, therefore, the messianic judge and the word of John can be paraphrased as follows: "God has made me strong (given me power) to proclaim the imminent judgment. As God's agent in this capacity, I prepare the way for another also authorized by God, whose strength (i.e. delegated power) so far exceeds mine that it makes the range of my authority seem like that of the lowest slave. This is because he will actually execute the judgment that I merely proclaim."

From what we have learned about John's conception of the judgment it must be clear that this messianic judge cannot be a human being. For analogies we must go instead to the angelic "manlike one" of Daniel 7, to whom power is given and who comes with the clouds of heaven.[18] Seen in the light of Daniel 7 the word about the Mightier One falls into line with John's proclamation about the nature of judgment and is beyond objection as a genuine utterance of the Baptist. Whatever be true about the point of view of the birth story, to which we shall return in another context, John's own proclamation must, therefore, have had two facets. It told of imminent judgment and of the coming of a messianic judge. In this particular it modified the eschatological picture of Malachi, where God himself judges, combining it with elements from Daniel. Whether still more has to be added to the picture an examination of the remaining saying about the two baptisms must show.

Like the word about the Mightier One, the saying that deals with the two baptisms comes to us in a number of different forms (Mk 1:8; Mt 3:11; Lk 3:16; Acts 1:5; 11:16; Jn 1:33). These it has developed in the course of a checkered career during which it changed from a saying of the Baptist to a word of Jesus and finally to an utterance of God himself addressed to the Baptist, in Acts and in the Fourth Gospel respectively. The differences between the variant forms can be ironed out readily, save in one particular.[19] In the second of the two correlative clauses of which the word is composed we have to choose between the form: "He will baptize you with Holy Spirit" (Mk, Acts and Jn) and "He will baptize you with Holy Spirit and with fire" (Mt and Lk). The choice has been complicated by the contention of some that Matthew's and Luke's form is a conflation of Mark and the Second Source, in which case we would have to postulate and cope with a third form, namely, "he will baptize you with fire."

Critics have dealt rather severely with the two forms of the saying actually preserved in our Gospel texts. They begin usually by pointing to John's conception of the Messiah as God's agent in judgment with which we are already familiar, and continue with a reference to the passage in Acts where certain "disciples" at Ephesus who have been baptized only with the baptism of John are said to be ignorant even of the existence of a Holy Spirit.

What room, they ask, is there for endowment with the Spirit by the Messiah in John's preaching under these circumstances? Finding no room, they interpret the Markan form of the saying, namely, "I baptize you with water, he will baptize you with Holy Spirit" as having been coined by the Church to show the contrast between the Christian and the Baptist rite. The form of Matthew and Luke, namely, "I baptize you with water, he will baptize you with Holy Spirit and with fire," they think of as having been inspired by the events of Pentecost. Hence, they normally give preference to the hypothetical third form supposedly found in the Second Source, namely, "he will baptize you with fire."[20] This can readily be interpreted as a metaphor of the fiery judgment and can be co-ordinated on this interpretation with what we know about the nature of judgment and the character and function of the Messiah in John's proclamation.

The interpretation has much to recommend it, once it has been formulated, but there are difficulties particularly in the procedure by which it is obtained. Three such difficulties are worthy of mention. The first concerns these people at Ephesus mentioned in Acts 19 to whom we shall return in a later context. Here it need only be said that what they did or did not know can scarcely be regarded as normative for the reconstruction of John's own thought. Even supposing that Acts has reported them correctly, they are themselves too enigmatic to clarify another enigma.[21] The second concerns the form of the saying "he will baptize you with fire." This, it will be recalled, is entirely hypothetical, being deduced from the agreement of Matthew and Luke against Mark. As a postulate, moreover, it lacks verisimilitude, for Matthew and Luke do not normally conflate Mark and the Second Source merely by adding the words of the one to those of the other, as they would have to have done had they derived from Mark's baptism "with Holy Spirit" and the Second Source's baptism "with fire" their own longer form, "with Holy Spirit and with fire." Finally, there is the difficulty provided by the distribution of the longer and shorter forms of the saying. Supposing that the longer form, "he will baptize you with Holy Spirit and with fire" was inspired by the events of Pentecost, it is strange that in Acts, where this association is indeed maintained, the short form, mentioning only the baptism "with Holy Spirit," is the one that is used. The sources thus demand for the Spirit a place in the earliest form of the saying but suggest no way of fitting the word into what is known about the Baptist's proclamation.

The traditional way of handling the problem thus posed is to assume that John did indeed visualize by prophetic insight a future development that would and eventually did bring about either a Pentecostal endowment with the Spirit as prophesied by Joel or a new rite of baptism that would supersede his own.[22] But this does violence to what else is known about John's messianic expectation and to the fundamental thesis of the birth story in which John is himself the agent of the eschatological consummation. It will not be amiss, therefore, to suggest a different solution and one that seems to do justice to both the historical circumstances and to the transmission of the evidence. This solution has its basis in a neglected connotation of the traditional Hebrew conception of the Spirit.

With our Christian upbringing we are inclined to think of God's Spirit as an inspiring and transforming power associated with the achievement of his creative and redemptive purposes. This is indeed an important part of the traditional Hebrew conception of the Spirit, but only a part. Even in the Synoptic Gospels, the basic function of the Spirit is twofold. The first is to empower men to witness to the truth, as when the Spirit descends on Jesus at baptism, or when men are said to speak in the Spirit. The second function is that of routing the forces of evil, as when Jesus in the Beelzebub controversy insists that it is not the prince of the demons but the Holy Spirit by which he drives out the demons (Mk 3:23–30), and when he implies that to deny the working of the Spirit in such acts is an unpardonable offense. This purgative and destructive aspect of the working of the Spirit (see also Mt 12:28) is as characteristic of the traditional Hebrew conception as the inspiring and uplifting function. It is obscured for us by our English translations which usually substitute the word "breath" for Spirit in such contexts, but, of course, in the Hebrew and the Aramaic there is no distinction between the words used. In eschatological contexts even of the New Testament period the one word Spirit (*pneuma*) can refer to the destructive workings of God's power quite as well as to its uplifting effects. So, for instance, in the famous apocalyptic passage in II Thessalonians 2:8, where we hear that the Messiah will destroy the Lawless One by the breath (*pneuma*) of his mouth, this being, of course, only an echo of statements such as that of Isaiah 11:4, "and with the breath (LXX: *pneuma*) of his lips shall he slay the wicked."

Following this line of thought it is possible to suggest that in the original saying of John which underlies the relevant New Testament material there was an allusion to the Spirit as a purgative and destructive force working through the Messiah. This saying, the tradition tells us, was taken over by the Christians and in certain circles was transformed into a word of Jesus and applied to the Pentecostal experiences (Acts). Here, then, the Spirit became the Holy Spirit and baptism with the Holy Spirit was interpreted as endowment with the spiritual gift of glossolaly and with the power of witness. In this application the verb "he will baptize" was still metaphorically used. Later, in other circles in which the Christian rite of baptism had come to be regarded as conferring the Holy Spirit, that is, the power of a new regenerate life, the saying of John was interpreted as a prophecy of the Christian rite and the verb was taken literally. This interpretation is probably the one reflected in the Gospel of Mark. Meanwhile, in still other Christian circles—circles less concerned with the phenomena of ecstatic religious experience or with the practice of the cult—the

effort was made to safeguard the word against misinter-
pretation. The safeguard was simple and epexegetical,
and consisted merely of the addition of the words "and
fire." This is to be understood as a hendyadys and is
intended to indicate that it is the "fiery" Spirit about
which John was speaking.[23] This is the form which the
Second Source has preserved.

All forms, then, are secondary, but when we interpret
them in the light of the possible circumstances of their
development we discover a basis for the evolution of the
series that has an intelligible word of John as its beginning. "In my baptism," John means to say, "I baptize
you with water for repentance, and if you repent not in
my baptism he, the Messiah, will destroy you with his
fiery breath or Spirit." So interpreted, the word of John
brings us face to face once more with the conception of
the transcendent Messiah as the agent of God's final judgment. Only one detail of this interpretation still remains
obscure, namely, how the destruction of the unrepentant
by the Messiah's fiery breath could be described as a baptism. The basis for the explanation of this detail has been
developed in exemplary fashion by C. M. Edsman and
the explanation, which is of the utmost importance for
the interpretation of John's own baptism, will be discussed in full in Chapter IV.[24]

This, then, is the burden of John's proclamation, the
imminence of the final universal judgment of God and
the coming of a transcendent Messiah whose function it
is to purge men of evil and to destroy the wicked. Not

since the days of Malachi had a message of such dire foreboding been proclaimed to the Jewish people, and not even in the days of Malachi had circumstances been as favorable to bring it home to those who heard.

It was in the deep trough of the Jordan valley, moreover, that John preached his message of doom. Enclosed by precipitous mountains that radiate the sun's heat, the valley that is pleasantly warm even in winter becomes a veritable inferno when the rains are past. Borne by the enervating southern winds this heat is like a breath from a furnace most of the year, withering and blasting all that is exposed to it.

In this inferno we must picture John the Baptist, a forbidding figure with unkempt beard and shaggy hair, his skin, bare save for loin-cloth and loose mantle, burned black by the relentless heat of the sun, his mind tortured by the thought of his people's offenses against an all-powerful and righteous God, spawning dire prophecies of doom and shrilling the cry of the coming day "that burneth like a furnace." Travelers along the dusty highroads that crossed the barren expanse, themselves fevered by the heat, found him thus, a terrifying figure with a terrifying message, dynamic, dramatic and either demonic or prophetic, depending on how they reacted to the burden of his words.

III

John's Preaching:
The Exhortation

ARLY Christian preaching, it would seem, had two
main elements, the *kerygma* or the proclamation
of the Gospel, and the *parenesis* or the exhortation. These
two elements are standard features of the missionary ad-
dresses with which the writer of Acts has studded his
book, and what the sermon outlines of Acts reveal has
its counterpart in the letters of Paul. At least the genuine
letters of Paul can usually be broken down into large
blocks of theological and ethical materials, and the probability that much of this material was used also in his
evangelistic work suggests that the great apostle to the
Gentiles made the same distinction between the proclamation and the exhortation in organizing his sermons.[1]

The presence of these two fixed elements in early
Christian preaching is not a matter of chance. The Gospel,
after all, was not a man-made affair, but a divine revelation concerning the meaning of certain events that had

taken place before the eyes of the original witnesses. Divinely revealed, it could not be argued; it could only be proclaimed. "We speak what we know and testify to what we have seen," says the Fourth Evangelist. But since the meaning of the events which the Gospel proclaimed was of final and decisive significance for the fate of men individually and collectively, the message was not one to which men could listen dispassionately. It called for action. Hence, the typical response to the proclamation is that described in the Book of Acts, where it is said of those who heard Peter's speech

> and they were pricked in their hearts and said to Peter and the rest of the disciples, Brethren, what shall we do? (Acts 2:37)

The exhortation is the necessary response to this query.

In its two types of subject matter Christian preaching is only the logical sequel to the preaching of John the Baptist. That John, too, uttered a proclamation fraught with crucial meaning for all men individually and collectively, we have already seen. It is not strange, therefore, that in Gospel record we should find the crowds, the publicans and even the soldiers coming to him with the question, What shall we do? (Lk 3:10), and that in this record we should find materials attributed to John that are of a hortatory character. It is this hortatory or ethical element of John's preaching that is our concern in this chapter.

Our knowledge of the hortatory part of John's preaching is meager, partly, no doubt, because its importance was eclipsed in the eyes of the Christians who transmitted it by the sayings of Jesus that had an ethical import. The evidence available consists of certain general statements summarizing John's exhortation, certain episodes of Gospel story involving allusions to the piety practiced by John's disciples, and a group of four specific words of John, addressed to the crowds, the publicans, the soldiers and to Herod Antipas respectively.

Among the general statements, the one that formulates John's exhortation most clearly is that of Matthew 3:1–2, where we are told that the Baptist came preaching in the wilderness, "Repent ye, for the Kingdom of Heaven is at hand." This is an elaboration of the Markan statement that John came preaching a baptism of repentance (Mk 1:4). Whether John actually used the expression Kingdom of God in his proclamation may be doubted, but the question is of no great importance for us, for the divine judgment that the Baptist proclaimed is, of course, the medium by which the all-powerful God establishes his eternal sovereignty. What *is* important is that in these summaries, as in the reply of Peter to the crowds at Pentecost, the word "repentance" is uniformly present and hence of basic significance.[2]

By giving repentance a significant place in his exhortation, John falls into line with the greatest of Israel's preachers since at least the days of Hosea. Inspired preaching, preaching that reflects a mind and a person overwhelmed with the experience of God's majesty and righteousness, must inevitably demand repentance as the expression of man's unworthiness before the face of God. At first national and, from Ezekiel on, also individual in character, repentance was clearly understood in Hebrew thought as the act by which men turned from sin and unrighteousness to God and to the performance of his will. In turning to God, the prophets had taught, Israel could obtain forgiveness, for God would surely pardon the iniquity of the repentant and cast his sins into the depths of the sea, as Micah had put it (Micah 7:18–20). By stressing God's willingness to forgive the repentant, the prophets of the Old Testament brought into sharp relief a contradiction that existed since the days of Amos and Hosea at least between the thought of God's absolute righteousness on the one hand and his mercy and love on the other. So far as forgiveness itself was concerned, Ezekiel clarified the contradiction by the famous declaration that God found no pleasure in the death of the wicked and desired only that man should turn from his sinful ways and live (Ezek 18:23). This meant that God's righteous anger was directed against sin rather than against the sinner, and gave the repentant grounds for believing that they would truly find merciful acceptance at God's hand. Yet the fact that in his mercy a righteous God did actually grant forgiveness of sins to the repentant was a source of never-ending wonder to the pious Jew and led him to extol not only the wonders of God's dealing with men but also the power and the greatness of repentance itself. Being a matter of such importance, repentance was inevitably given sharp definition in Jewish thought. It was clearly understood to involve not only the attitude of contrition in respect to the past and the confession by the repentant of his guilt, but also, on the positive side, the effort to live acceptably in God's sight by the performance of the demands of God's holy will.[3] The question is whether John in his conception of repentance differed in any way from what the prophets of the Old Testament and the rabbis of his day said on this point.

In the association of repentance with baptism Lohmeyer has recently found a basis for asserting that John's conception of repentance did differ fundamentally from that of contemporary Judaism. Starting from the assumption that in John's thought baptism was the divinely revealed medium for man's rebirth, he concludes that to save men in connection with baptism repentance must involve first an acceptance of baptism as the revealed instrument of regeneration, and secondly the experience in baptism of entrance into a new type of being. Repentance, therefore, is not merely a reorientation of the human will associated with baptism, but more specifically a change in man's being through the gift of revealed insight and of rebirth.[4]

If true, this interpretation would actually set John's conception of repentance apart from anything known to contemporary Judaism. It is to be feared, however, that the interpretation owes more to the premises of a dialectical theology and to its tendency to transform an eschatological crisis into a subjective process than to the consideration of historical probabilities. Two things have to be admitted in taking this adverse position. The first is that repentance is nowhere defined in the New Testament, whether by John, Jesus or the Christian writers. The second is that the God-fearing Jew can and does pray to the Lord to make him truly repentant, and thereby acknowledges his complete dependence upon the divine initiative. Yet the first of these facts probably implies only that the nature and content of repentance could be taken for granted because it was interpreted in traditional terms, while the second suggests only a healthy reverence for God's assistance in *all* that men achieve, and does not in the least imply the inability of the human will to assert itself actively, in this case to perform the act of repentance.[5] Indeed, only because it involves the action of man's own will can repentance be regarded in Jewish circles as the condition *sine qua non* of the efficacy of all ritual expiations, including those of the Day of Atonement.[6] So far as John is concerned, it would seem improper to read into his thought the premises of a dialectical theology not only because this would remove him from the historical context to which he so clearly belongs, but also because it would make Jesus's reaction to him unintelligible. Jesus, it must be recalled, participated in John's baptism of repentance, yet he did not choose to perpetuate it after John's death, or to make it the criterion of men's acceptance before God. This would have been impossible had repentance had for John the connotations that Lohmeyer assigns to it.

THE EXHORTATION

It seems wise, therefore, to assume that for John repentance had the same basic meaning as for all Jews, namely, that of turning from sin in contrition and confession, and of turning to the will of God. Only in two particulars can we say that John modified the conception, namely, first in the urgency that he attached to it, and second in the way in which he associated it with baptism. The urgency arises naturally from the connection between the exhortation to repent and the proclamation of an imminent judgment, and requires no further discussion. The association with baptism tells us something about the nature of the baptism, as we shall see in another context, but is important to us here because it shows that repentance for John must come to expression in concrete acts, and one such act, an act of especial importance, was the act of being baptized.

This same emphasis upon the positive aspects of repentance we find repeated in the first of the four hortatory sayings, namely, the word:

> Produce fruit worthy of repentance and do not think to say, "We have Abraham for our father," for I tell you God can raise up children to Abraham from these stones. (Mt 3:8–9; Lk 3:8)[7]

If John here speaks of fruit of repentance, he is referring metaphorically to acts exhibiting the repentance, quite as Paul, in speaking of the "fruit of the Spirit" refers to acts of love, joy, peace, long-suffering, gentleness, goodness and faith, inspired by the Spirit. Two points are made in connection with John's demand for such acts. The first is that they should be worthy, and the second that certain considerations of Abrahamic descent should not prevent their appearance. The first of these two points involves no obscurity. To be worthy the acts called for must express the worth and value of repentance itself. Now it is clear from contemporary utterance that repentance was regarded as having in God's sight a value second to none among the acts of men. For this reason it was commonly said that the prayer of a repentant sinner enjoyed priority in coming to God's attention over all other petitions addressed to the Almighty, and for this reason, too, Jesus declared that there would be more joy in heaven over one sinner who repented than over ninety-nine righteous persons needing no repentance (Lk 15:7).[8] To be worthy of repentance, the acts of human piety called for by John in this saying would, therefore, need to be of the same exemplary character and value in God's sight as repentance itself. Once this is understood, the warning against the considerations which should not be permitted to prevent their appearance can be seen in its proper setting.

John's warning, "Do not think to say, We have Abraham for our father," has sometimes been interpreted to mean that race is not a basis for claims to exemption from repentance expressed in worthy acts. This interpretation probably goes too far, imputing to John the removal of the distinctions between Jew and Gentile that appear for the first time in so many words in the letters

72

of Paul. What discredits this interpretation is its inability to cope with the statement that God is able to raise up children to Abraham from the myriad stones of the countryside. What God can conceivably do is not immediately relevant to the assertion that he does not accept race as a criterion. Nor is it clear why, if John has just affirmed that Abrahamic descent does not count, he should now speak of God creating a new progeny for the selfsame Abraham. This would only weaken the force of the original declaration.[9]

John's reference to the children that God might conceivably raise up to Abraham is, therefore, better taken to imply that there was present in the patriarch some particular value so great that God would be sure to preserve it even if it meant creating an entirely new Israelite people, to take the place of the old. The real question, then, is what significance the patriarch had that might, if necessary, impel God to such a course of action. Attention has been called in this connection to the Pauline conception of Abraham as the hero of faith and the spiritual ancestor of the believer. Like Paul, it is said, John is urging his hearers to see in faith the proper response to the revelation of baptism as the divinely ordained means of salvation, and thus to imitate Abraham whose faith rather than his works were credited to him for righteousness.[10] This interpretation is the necessary corollary of the dialectical conception of repentance already discussed and shares with it the latter's limitations. To read the Pauline theology back into the sayings of the Baptist in this way is not only to commit an historical blunder but also to forget that the saying begins with the injunction to produce fruits worthy of repentance.

Under these circumstances it is much better to assume that the reference to the children that God might conceivably raise up to Abraham involves a criticism of Jews who relied upon the merits of the patriarch for their salvation instead of acquiring merit for themselves by pious observance.[11] God might well be thought to disown and to replace them with others who would not abuse the doctrine of merit and would not in so doing show disrespect of the divine mercy. But one fact has to be kept in mind if this approach to the saying is followed, namely, that the merit of Abraham derived from his having done more in the expression of his piety than God demanded and later set forth in the Law. If, therefore, John is urging his hearers to perform acts commensurate in importance with the outstanding act of repentance, the criticism of those who rely on Abrahamic sonship involves not so much their failure to obey the commands of the Law as their unwillingness to go beyond the Law as Abraham had done. The saying, then, really turns about a "more" which John demanded, a "more" fit to be associated with the act of repentance. This more the Jews rejected saying, "We recognize the need for repentance and for the observance of the Law. If these are not enough to save us, we know we may fall back upon the supererogatory merit of the patriarch. Why then should we regard as normative for us the 'more' which you demand?" To this John's answer was, "You should do the 'more' precisely because you are supposed to be the descendants of Abraham, who himself did more than the Law subsequently demanded. Only he who does this 'more' is worthy to be called a son of Abraham."

Our study of John's exhortation thus far has led us to affirm that the Baptist stressed in his preaching the need for individual repentance, and that he demanded of those who would be saved an exemplary piety analogous to that of Abraham. This the eschatological crisis set forth in his proclamation may truly be said to require. The only question is, can we specify the nature of the "more" which John demanded?

One element of the "more" is undoubtedly baptism itself. Baptism was for John, as we have seen, an act expressing repentance, but one which was not enjoined in the Law. If John came preaching a baptism of repentance as a requirement for escape from the terrors of judgment, his demand posed a real problem not so much to those who were careless about the fulfillment of God's Law, but rather to those who believed that in the Law the complete will of God was revealed. If the Law contained the complete expression of God's will and yet did not mention baptism, what was the validity of John's demand? We still catch glimpses of the debates which the "more" of baptism occasioned among the more intelligent both in the catch question which Jesus posed at Jerusalem when he asked whether John's baptism was from heaven or of men; that is, whether it had divine sanction and hence was obligatory or not (Mk 11:30), and in the story dimly reported by the Fourth Evangelist about a discussion between some of John's disciples and a Jew about purification (Jn 3:25).[12] To the debates on the validity of John's demand for a "more" of baptism, the saying exhorting the Jews to exemplary acts just because they are descendants of Abraham is a fitting reply.

Two other elements of the "more" which John demanded are revealed in random incidents from the life of Jesus preserved in our Gospels. They are fasting and prayer respectively.

What we hear about Baptist fasting applies, strictly speaking, to the disciples of John, but can with complete propriety be related to John himself. The familiar passage in Mark tells us merely that

> John's disciples and the Pharisees were fasting and they come and say to him (namely Jesus), Why do John's disciples and the disciples of the Pharisees fast, but thy disciples do not fast? (Mk 2:18)[13]

Precisely what the fasting practice of the Baptist groups may have been we do not know. It may be the Pharisaic practice of fasting twice a week on Mondays and Thursdays, to which reference is made in the familiar Parable of the Publican and the Pharisee (Lk 18:12). Or again it may be a seasonal fast, which happened to overlap with the bi-weekly fast of the Pharisees when the question

about Jesus' disciples not fasting was raised. In all probability, however, it was fasting in excess of that demanded
by the Law, for instance in connection with the Day of
Atonement; otherwise, Jesus' disciples would have been
fasting also.[14]

Fasting in excess of the demands of the Law as practiced by individuals and groups in later Judaism had
various motives. Fundamentally the motives were not
ascetic. There was nothing intrinsically objectionable in
the food from which people abstained, and nothing about
the human body that required its mortification. Occa-
sionally, it seems, the extension of the fasting practice
was purely disciplinary, serving merely to give the faster
the assurance that he could actually do all the Law demanded because he could do more. Frequently, however,
excess fasting is interpreted as an expression of repentance,
as, for instance, in the Testaments of the Twelve Patriarchs, where the patriarchal heroes are regularly described as exhibiting their penitence individually in long
fasts. Indeed, in contemporary thought we find the belief
that those who fast in excess of the demands of the Law,
do a particular service to their nation. They represent
the nation before God in its ideal state and in so doing
impel him to overlook the deficiencies of other individuals
and to be gracious to the nation as a whole. Here fasting
becomes vicarious in its significance.[15]

What has been said about the function of non-ob-
ligatory fasting in later Judaism provides all that we need
to explain its appearance in Baptist piety. For John, we

may suppose, such fasting was also associated with repentance, bringing that repentance to expression in concrete acts. Being like baptism in excess of the Law, fasting shared with baptism the exemplary character that made it worthy of repentance. Since contemporary thought connected it with the patriarchs, it could be recommended with the injunction that claims to Abrahamic descent must find expression in the exemplary piety of the forefathers. Indeed, if the final judgment impending left the fate of the nation in the balance, exemplary acts of fasting vicarious in their import were a dire necessity if God was to spare any of the trees of the orchard that symbolized the Chosen People.

What we know about Baptist prayer is quite as meager as what we know about Baptist fasting. The evidence is limited virtually to the request which Jesus' disciples addressed to their Lord, namely,

> Lord, teach us to pray even as John also taught his disciples (Lk 11:1).[16]

The request is necessarily good historical evidence, for later generations would scarcely have been inclined to suggest that the Lord's Prayer was given to assimilate Christian to Baptist piety.

When the disciples of Jesus speak of prayer among the Baptist's followers, the reference is naturally not to the standard forms of private and public prayer commonly in use by all Jews at the time. Whatever the daily prayer customs of pious Jews were at the time, the repetition twice daily of the Shema, the use of prayer at meals, the recitation of an early form of the Amidah at synagogue in the morning and the afternoon, John did not have to instruct his disciples in them any more than Jesus did. Rather, the reference must be to special prayers formulated by the Baptist himself for use by his disciples in addition to those commonly spoken by their compatriots. All we know about them is that Luke in another context (5:33) calls them *deeseis;* that is, prayers of petition and supplication, and that the Lord's Prayer, given to the Christian disciples as a counterpart of such Baptist prayers, is also petitional in character. Indeed, if we set the Lord's Prayer against the background of John's proclamation, there is little in it that could not have been made the subject of petition in Baptist circles quite as appropriately as in Christian circles. The emphasis upon the eschatological consummation in the petition for the coming of the kingdom, and the request for divine forgiveness and deliverance—these, at least, must have been common to what John and Jesus taught their disciples to pray.

To understand the function which such supplementary prayer usage had in Baptist circles, we must fall back again upon our knowledge of contemporary Judaism. From what we know about contemporary Judaism it is evident that, whatever other needs they may have satisfied, the special prayers of individuals and groups served to express particularly the attitude of repentance. This is evident in part, at least, from the large number of penitential prayers and psalms preserved in the literature of later Judaism. Besides serving to express repentance, individual prayer was also commonly associated with fasting, so much so that for certain types of fasting the designation "prayer-fast" was current.[17] A textual variant of great antiquity in Mark 9:29 has Jesus himself testify to this association when he declares that certain types of demons can be exorcised only by prayer and fasting.

The association of prayer and fasting with each other, the association of both with repentance and the association of repentance with baptism, show that we have in these aspects of Baptist piety, in all probability, a unified program of religious action. In laying this program upon his nation, John apparently exhorted the nation to realize that the imminence of the final judgment called for a supreme effort. The effort must be to transcend the piety of obligation by the voluntary performance of acts of exemplary piety in which repentance could be brought to positive expression. In the necessity for such repentance he probably saw the authorization for the "more" which he specified and by which he set himself apart from the other religious leaders of his day.

Of this interpretation of the central theme of John's exhortation we have two confirming testimonies. The first is the emphasis which Josephus puts on the cleansing of the soul by righteous conduct in his simplified version of the Baptist's preaching.[18] The second is a passage in Matthew, where Jesus says to the chief priests and elders,

John came unto you in the way of righteousness, and
ye believed him not; but the publicans and the har-
lots believed him; and ye, when ye saw it, did not
even repent yourselves afterward, that ye might believe. (Mt 21:32)

In this saying Jesus characterizes John not as a prophet,
not as Elijah, but as one who came in the way of righteousness, that is as one who taught acceptability before
God in terms of the performance of righteous acts. That
being true, a people steeped in observantism should have
understood and accepted him. Yet his preaching, making
certain extraordinary demands not enjoined in the Law,
involved acceptance of him as one authorized to make
such demands. The "chief priests and elders" did not believe that he was divinely authorized. Nor did they revise
their judgment when the religiously ostracized circles
accepted him and reformed, thereby demonstrating that
God's power was working through him. In Jesus' opinion
the "chief priests and elders" had forfeited their claim
to pre-eminence and leadership by virtue of this fact.

While seeking, as we have seen, to rouse men to extraordinary acts of piety, John naturally did not neg-
lect to inculcate those basic ethical standards which the
prophets of the Old Testament saw in God and required
of men. Of this we have evidence in the three sayings
preserved by Luke alone and addressed respectively to
the crowds, certain publicans and certain elements of the
local mercenary soldiery. To the crowds John says:

> Whoever has two shirts, let him share with him who has none, and whoever has food, let him do likewise.

To the publicans:

> Exact no more than the established tax rate allows.

And to the soldiers:

> Do not apply violence for personal gain; do not lay false charges; and be satisfied with your wages. (Lk 3:11–14)

That publicans were inclined to charge all the traffic would bear, and that soldiers possessing in their weapons the means of physical compulsion sometimes took advantage of their position to add to their income by intimidation and threat of denunciation was common knowledge. This was rehearsed to point out that power is abused where personal gain is given primary consideration. The sayings are, therefore, in no sense obscure and require no extensive comment.[19] What does invite comment is the fact that in these injunctions there is visible no disposition to change the basic conditions of life in the face of the eschatological crisis, and no attempt to distinguish between suitable and unsuitable vocations. All these things, it is assumed, may remain as they are. John is concerned only that men, whatever their station in life, shall exhibit in their lives the basic virtues of sharing, of integrity, and honesty—in short, of probity and comity in social relationships. This is the traditional pattern of righteousness

developed by a law-abiding Judaism under the influence
of ethical monotheism.

Seen from the angle of his exhortation with its roots
in the traditional pattern of righteous acts, and its crown
in the demand for an exemplary "more" of repentance,
John's fundamental significance cannot be stated better
than in the words of the angel announcing his birth,
namely:

> He will turn many of the children of Israel to the
>   Lord their God
> And he will go before him with the spirit and the
>   power of Elijah,
> To turn the affections of the fathers to the children,
> And to fill the disobedient with the wisdom of the
>   just,—
> To make ready for the Lord a prepared people.
>   (Lk 1:16–17)

Of the several statements made by the angel in this
annunciation, that which speaks of John having the spirit
and power of Elijah can be further elucidated by the one
saying of the Baptist that still remains to be discussed.
This is the denunciatory saying of ethical import publicly
addressed by John to Herod Antipas,

> It is not lawful for thee to have thy brother's wife.
>   (Mk 6:18)

The circumstances which provoked this utterance are
made thoroughly clear both by Mark, who first recorded

it, and by the information concerning the life of Herod
Antipas supplied by the Jewish historian Josephus.
Herodias, the woman in question, was the daughter of
Antipas' half-brother Aristobulus. No odium was attached to the fact that by marrying her, Antipas was
espousing his own niece. Nor was it legally reprehensible
that to marry her he had to divorce an earlier wife, a
Nabatæan princess, the daughter of King Aretas IV.
What was objectionable was that this Herodias had been
the wife of still another half-brother, a certain Herod.[20]
For Antipas to marry her was a direct contravention of
the ordinance of Leviticus 20:21, "If a man shall take
his brother's wife, it is impurity." Sanction was given to
such sister-in-law marriage by Jewish law only under the
condition that the brother had died and had died without
issue. In such cases, by the law of Levirite marriage, it
actually became the duty of a surviving brother to marry
the wife of the deceased, to raise up children to him.
But in this case the obscure half-brother Herod was still
alive, and what is more, Herodias had borne him a
daughter, the famous dancing maiden of Mark 6:22. According to Jewish law, therefore, the Baptist's charge was
strictly in order. On the part of John, however, it was
more than merely "in order." For one who had come
teaching "the way of righteousness" and demanding of
men exemplary acts of piety, the spectacle of men in high
places flaunting the Law's authority must have been
highly provocative. Fearless as he was in his denunciation of the priesthood, whom he called a "brood of vipers,"

John could be counted on not to let Antipas' action pass without calling him to account.

John's denunciation of Antipas is reported parenthetically by Mark in the familiar story of the Baptist's execution. It will not be amiss to treat the rest of the story in the present context, for the chain of events to which the denunciation gave rise throws still further light on the character of John's exhortation.

Of the circumstances of John's imprisonment and death we have two accounts. The one is the familiar story of Mark 6, the other, the less familiar account of Josephus. The two accounts differ significantly. Josephus' account is brief indeed. He merely indicates that Antipas feared John's hold upon the Jewish people and suspected him of designs to foment a political insurrection. By reason of his suspicion he thought it wise to forestall any revolutionary movement that might be planned by removing John from the scene. In consequence, John was imprisoned in the fortress of Machærus and there beheaded.[21] *John Imprisonment & death 28 & early 29 A.D.*

The conception of John as a potential leader of a political revolt, imputed by Josephus to Antipas in this account, is one for which the reader of the Gospels is ill-prepared. There is virtually nothing in the material which we have studied that might be said to have political implications. The only possible exception is the word of John about the Mightier One, which could conceivably have been misconstrued and given a political turn, quite as a certain word of Jesus about the destruction of the

Temple was misconstrued and used against him in his trial (Mk 14:58). But his accusers got nowhere with Jesus' word about the Temple, and it is not likely that John's word about the Mightier One would have provided a better basis for preferring charges against the Baptist. The question is, therefore, whether Josephus is imagining things and has completely misinterpreted the circumstances of John's death.

Turning from Josephus to Mark we find that in Gospel story the account of John's execution lacks all traces of political overtones and turns upon the private grudge of a woman, Herod's second wife, Herodias. Herodias, we are told, "had it in" for John because of what he had said about Antipas' second marriage. With her upbringing in the Medici-like environment of the Herodian courts, she would have contrived to bring about John's unobtrusive disappearance from the scene had not her husband interfered, by putting John into protective custody. Even that, however, did not permanently thwart her, for, watching her opportunities and taking Antipas unawares through the agency of her daughter at the occasion of the famous banquet, she brought about the fulfillment of her schemes.

The story gives what must be regarded as an excellent characterization of Herodias. It is precisely in the role in which Mark casts her—an opportunist, a wily schemer, a woman motivated by deep-seated jealousies and overvaulting ambitions, a veritable Lady Macbeth—that she appears in the pages of Josephus. Only a few years later we find her roused to such envy by Agrippa's advancement to royal rank that she urges Antipas on to claim similar advancement for himself at Rome, and thereby brings about his and her own downfall.

With all this excellent portrayal of Herodias, the story is nonetheless open to suspicion of inaccuracy and invention at many points. Herodias was in all probability not really the wife of Antipas' brother Philip, as Mark says, but of the half-brother Herod, as we have already seen. Her dancing daughter was scarcely at this time still a maiden, as Mark says, but already in all probability the wife of the Tetrarch Philip. Antipas' promise to Salome of "half his kingdom" has all the earmarks of the fairy-tale, especially since he had no kingdom and what he had was not his to give, and the presence of a respectable woman, particularly a daughter of a noble family, at an ancient stag dinner is quite unlikely. The characterization of Herod, too, is full of difficulties. He appears in Mark's account as the enlightened Hellenistic monarch, the friend and patron of prophets, and, we must imagine, of philosophers, artists and men of letters. Hence, he tries to rescue John from the machinations of Herodias, and summons John to discourse before him on his special themes. Such enlightened patronage as is involved in Herod's "hearing John gladly," would doubtless have been more than John could have borne. What is more to the point, there is no possible way of reconciling Antipas' "protective custody" of John as related by Mark, and his consequent "grief" at being outwitted by Hero-

dias, with Josephus' account of the Baptist's removal
because of a threat to Antipas' own sovereignty. Virtually
all that remains of Mark's account is, therefore, the characterization of the several persons and John's denunciation of Antipas, which, as we have already seen, has all
the ear-marks of authenticity. Our problem, then, is how
to reconcile the two conflicting stories, each of which has
its own difficulties and intangibles, and so to gain some
idea of the circumstances involved in John's execution.

It is important in this connection to have a clear picture of the circumstances of Antipas' first marriage, and
of the effects of its dissolution. Antipas' first wife, we
have already said, was an Oriental princess, the daughter of the Nabatæan king Aretas IV. To those familiar
with the political and cultural history of the Near East
in New Testament times, the importance of this fact will
be evident at once. Of all the lesser kingdoms of the
Near East at this time, the Nabatæan was, without
doubt, intrinsically the strongest and economcially the
most favored.[22] Modern exploration and excavation have
brought this ever more clearly into view. Established by
the unification of nomadic Arab tribes that had settled
in the eastern and southern parts of Palestine as early
as the fifth century B.C., the kingdom included in the New
Testament period a vast territory that extended from the
frontiers of Egypt and Palestine on the south, through
most of what is now Hashemite Transjordan, northward to the region of Damascus, saving only the free
cities of the Decapolis, the narrow strip in the Jordan

valley that was Antipas' Peræa, and the tetrarchy of Philip beyond the Lake of Galilee. Strategically placed for the conduct of caravan traffic over the long routes to the inner Orient, the kingdom became extremely wealthy, creating in its capital city of Petra a lasting monument to its affluence and its aspirations to Hellenistic culture. At the same time, because of its hold upon the nomadic tribes of the Transjordan countryside and the desert fringe, it was able to put into the field large armies noted for their fighting prowess. With its economic strength and its military might, it was the natural rival to the kingdom that Herod the Great had carved out for himself and that was now divided among his three sons, all of them weaklings compared with their father and the then-reigning Nabatæan king, Aretas IV. One of Antipas' possessions, it will be recalled, was Peræa, that narrow strip of territory along the east bank of the Jordan river, almost completely surrounded by Nabatæan spheres of influence, inhabited by a population that had strong Arabic admixtures, and open to the infiltration in winter of more nomadic Arab elements. For Antipas as the ruler of Peræa to ally himself by marriage to the royal Nabatæan house was, under these circumstances, a wise move and the best guarantee of the stability of his reign. By the same token, a rift in this marital alliance was fraught with the gravest consequences of a political nature for Antipas.

What happened when Antipas decided to divorce his wife, the Nabatæan princess, in order to marry Herodias,

Josephus tells us in full. It appears that the princess got wind of the arrangements that were being made to divorce her, and anticipated Antipas' action by a clever stratagem. Quite casually she asked her husband's permission to visit the fortress of Machærus, the southernmost outpost of Peræa overlooking the Dead Sea near the frontier between Peræa and the kingdom of her father. From here she was spirited away, no doubt by her father's henchman, and escaped to the Nabatæan court, probably at Petra. Antipas' plan to divorce her, duly retailed to her fond parent, was interpreted by him as an insult to the royal Nabatæan household which could not be left unavenged. Within a few years a war broke out between Aretas and Antipas in which Antipas' lands were invaded and his troops were defeated. The Nabatæans would have run him out of his tetrarchy had the Romans not stepped in and called a halt.[23]

A knowledge of the political complications involved in Antipas' marital adventures is of some importance for the interpretation of the circumstances that led to the Baptist's death. Josephus tells us that Antipas' defeat at Nabatæan hands was commonly regarded by the Jewish people as a punishment divinely visited upon the tetrarch for his murder of John. But there is more to the picture than this detail. In view of the explosive situation created by the flight of the Nabatæan princess, the sudden appearance of a man in the Jordan valley and in Peræa publicly denouncing Antipas and saying, "It is not lawful for thee to have thy brother's wife" was not only

embarrassing, it was politically explosive. It meant align-
ing the pious Jewish inhabitants of Peræa with those
of Arabic stock against their sovereign and thus foment-
ing sedition and encouraging insurrection. John's denunciation of Antipas as reported in Mark, far from con-
tradicting Josephus, provides the one detail necessary to
make Josephus' account of the political threat involved
in the Baptist's exhortation intelligible.

John's involvement in the national affairs of his day
as borne out by the combined testimony of Mark and
Josephus, throws into bold relief a side of the Baptist's
activity often not sufficiently appreciated. We have already suggested in another context that his preaching
included words of bitter denunciation addressed to the
priesthood of Jerusalem. Here we see his opposition extending itself to the political rulers. Far from seeking
eremitic seclusion, John, with his protest against urban
life, his demands for an active expression of repentance in
acts of higher righteousness, with his counsels of wisdom
to crowds, tax-collectors and soldiery, and with his fearless denunciation of wickedness in high places, appears
rather as a man who struggled mightily to turn the current of national life in his day and generation. This, his
proclamation of a final judgment beginning with the trees
of the orchard may well be said to have motivated. More
important in the present context is the fact that his stern
words addressed to Herod Antipas automatically place
John in a succession of men of God who, in earlier, more
outspoken, days, had ventured to act as censors of royal

acts. The Old Testament is full of stories of men of this type, men like Samuel in the days of Saul, like Nathan in the days of David, like Ahijah in the days of Jeroboam and like Jeremiah in the days of Josiah, Jehoiakim and Zedekiah. Among them all the most colorful is perhaps Elijah, who carried on the bitter feud with Ahab and Jezebel. No wonder, then, that John, with his wilderness life and dress, his demand for a final decision between two alternatives, repentance or destruction, with his bold affront to the political and religious leaders of his people, and, it should be noted, with his sudden appearance in the very region from which the fiery chariot was said to have taken the prophet to heaven (II Kgs 2:1–8), was believed to be Elijah himself returned to earth.

Concerning the place where the Baptist was incarcerated and executed, there is a measure of contradiction between our sources. Mark with his story of the birthday feast at which the Tetrarch Antipas was entertaining the higher dignitaries of the court, the army and the prominent citizens of Galilee, clearly implies that John was imprisoned and executed in the royal palace at Tiberias on the Lake of Galilee.[24] So interpreted, Mark contradicts Josephus, who relates that John was imprisoned and executed at the frontier fortress of Machærus on the shore of the Dead Sea.[25] Of the two accounts the latter is for various reasons the more probable. As long as John remained on the western bank of the Jordan, in Judæa or in Samaria, he was, of course, quite safe from the enmity of Antipas. But, as we have already seen, John also baptized on the eastern bank of the river, near Bethany across the Jordan. Here he was in Antipas' bailiwick, Peræa, just a few kilometers beyond the northern end of the Dead Sea. It must have been at the occasion of a sojourn in this area that John was taken prisoner on orders from Antipas. That being so, the chances are that he was taken to the nearby Machærus, which probably served as military headquarters for the region, and there executed.

The chronological limits of John's activity as a figure of public note are difficult to fix. Our only evidence is the statement of Luke that John received his "call" as a prophet in the fifteenth year of the Emperor Tiberius (Lk 3:1–2), and Mark's observation that after John had been "handed over," that is, imprisoned or executed, Jesus appeared upon the scene in Galilee as a preacher (Mk 1:14). The accuracy of both statements has been questioned, particularly by Robert Eisler, who has tried to show that John died in 35 A.D., a number of years after the crucifixion of Jesus.[26] This terminal date, arrived at by the use of the "Slavonic" Josephus and the outbreak of the war between Aretas and Antipas, cannot be held against the testimony of the Gospels. If, as seems most likely though by no means absolutely certain, Jesus was crucified in 30 A.D. after a ministry of one year plus, John's imprisonment and death must be placed late in the year 28 or early in 29 A.D. This would seem at first glance to conflict with Luke's statement that the call came to John in the fifteenth year of Tiberius, for

Tiberius' reign began in the late summer of 14 A.D. To date an event by assigning it to an emperor's regnal year is unusual in Roman times. It is largely an inherited Oriental practice and leaves an element of uncertainty because the system of calculation differs from place to place, as the evidence of the coins clearly shows. We do not know what system of counting Luke used in his famous synchronisms, but the likeliest is the Syrian, which would yield the date 27–28 A.D. as equivalent of the fifteenth year of Tiberius. For John, too, we are therefore able to allow only one year plus as the probable duration of his public career.[27]

John's career, then, was meteoric. Suddenly he appeared upon the horizon, and quite as suddenly he was gone again, but during the brief period of his sojourn he burned with the white heat of prophetic passion, heralding once more the imminent judgment of God and exhorting men with words of encouragement and denunciation to repent, not only in word but in deeds of exemplary piety. When he departed from the scene John left behind him a new rite, the rite of baptism, a successor who was to enshrine his memory in the hearts of distant generations, and a community of disciples who devoutly followed his preaching of the "way of righteousness." What they tell us about John forms the subject matter of the following chapters.

IV

John's Rite of Baptism

IN the eyes of John's contemporaries the rite he performed was undoubtedly the outstanding feature of his movement. This, the name "Baptizer" or "Baptist" applied to him in Jewish and Christian circles, clearly indicates.[1] Without a full discussion of this rite no treatment of John the Baptist would, therefore, be complete. But it is more than our knowledge of John that is at stake here. John's baptism became in the natural course of events the forerunner of another rite, the rite of Christian baptism, which has survived in the Church to the present day, and which constitutes for us as Christians a part of our own religious heritage. Because baptism is a part of our heritage, it is something the nature and significance of which we need to understand, and for that understanding a clear conception of its origin and antecedents is essential. Hence, it is with particular interest that we turn to a study of John's rite, the forebear of our own sacrament.

What is for us as Christians a matter of particular interest is also for us as students of history a matter of prime importance. Much can and has already been said in the preceding chapters about John's personal life, about his proclamation and about his exhortation. All these things are highly significant. But in the phenomenology of religion we often learn as much about the intrinsic character of a religious movement from its rite and ritual as we do from the person and utterances of its founder. This is because rite and ritual, corresponding to the need of the human individual for the dramatization of his devotion, often express with particular clarity the inner compulsions of his religious belief. Yet the very fact that rites are so important as the media for the expression of belief is often the source of difficulty to the historian who would discover their original meaning. This is because they tend to change their meaning in the natural course of events, making it no easy matter to determine what the basic core of the whole development may have been. We must proceed carefully, therefore, with due attention to all the available evidence if we are to interpret correctly the fundamental import of John's baptismal rite.

The primary data available in the sources for our knowledge of the nature of John's baptism are meager. From the references to the places where he baptized, namely, the Jordan and the springs at Ænon near Salim, and from the account of Jesus' baptism at the hands of John it is evident that we are dealing with a rite performed in the open in running water. The Greek word "baptize," translating the Aramaic *tebal*, implies furthermore that the action of the rite is a "dipping" or "bathing," whose function it is to apply to the entire body.[2] Immersion is thus the natural implication of the terminology and must be regarded as the normal procedure in the original performance of the rite. Whether in John's baptism the individual immersed himself or was immersed by the Baptist is not entirely clear, but certainly the act of immersion took place in the presence and under the direction of a celebrant, namely, John himself, who for this reason was called the Baptizer, or the Baptist.[3] Doubtlessly, prayers and benedictions accompanied the act, but of these we have no direct information. Only the statement of Mark, that the people were baptized "confessing their sins" (Mk 1:5), may contain a reminiscence of such liturgical adjuncts of the rite.

Equally fragmentary is the information available concerning the meaning of John's baptism. We have, under this heading, three bits of relevant material. The first is the saying of John about the two baptisms, in which John's water rite is contrasted to baptism with Spirit and fire (Mk 1:8; Mt 3:11; Lk 3:16). The second is the statement of Mark that John came preaching a baptism of repentance for the remission of sins (Mk 1:4). The third is the statement of Josephus that, in urging the Jews to come together to baptism, John intended baptism to be used, not to beg off from sins committed, but rather for the purification of the body, the soul having previously been cleansed by righteous conduct.[4] All three statements are important and must be accounted for in any explanation of the meaning of the rite, but they are not in themselves, alone or as a group, particularly enlightening. For one thing, it is not immediately clear wherein the contrast between water baptism and baptism with Spirit and fire lies. In the same way, it is not evident precisely what the relation of baptism and repentance really is; that is, whether baptism confers the forgiveness of sins or is only associated with an act of forgiveness on God's part. Finally there is a measure of contradiction between Josephus' statement that baptism was not used by John "to beg off from sins committed" serving rather to purify the body, and Mark's description of it as an act of repentance for the remission of sins.

The element of ambiguity and contradiction contained in these statements has led scholars to approach the problem of the meaning of John's rite from an entirely different angle. Given the fact that the Baptist rite is the forebear of Christian baptism and having some idea of the meaning of the latter, they endeavor to state the meaning of the former in such a way as to make intelligible a development leading from the former toward the latter. Usually this genetic approach involves the use of still a third element, namely, a hypothetical source for John's ceremony in which the germ for the whole development, Baptist and Christian alike, may be said to lie. The procedure thus followed is entirely legitimate and has much to recommend it providing the antecedent and the terminal factors of the process can really be brought into harmony. Now Christian baptism, which is the terminal feature of the development, may be said to have in our New Testament documents a twofold meaning. The first is that of an initiatory rite by means of which the convert becomes a member of the Christian community and eventually receives as a distinguishing feature of his status the gift of the Holy Spirit. The second is that of a rite of participation in the soteriological process, whether as an act of rebirth out of water and spirit or as an act of participation in the death and resurrection of Jesus. Recent attempts to ascertain the meaning of John's baptism by the use of the genetic approach have taken their cue from one or the other of these features of the Christian sequel. They thus fall into two groups, with each of which we shall have briefly to concern ourselves. The first group, starting from the initiatory aspect of the Christian sequel, looks to an initiatory immersion as the antecedent for the whole Baptist-Christian development, and takes recourse to the Jewish rite of proselyte baptism as that which will help us to understand the meaning of John's baptism. The question is whether and how adequately antecedent and sequel can be brought into line on this assumption.

Christian scholars, when they first began to discuss proselyte baptism, spoke of it as a Jewish imitation of Christian baptism, but a growing sense of historical proportion soon showed how impossible this conception was. Subsequently there developed a controversy over whether proselyte baptism was practiced early enough to serve as a prototype of John's baptism. The opinions aired and the evidence presented in the course of this controversy have made it clear that ablutions commonly called "proselyte baptism" were actually in use at a date sufficiently early to have served as such a prototype if the Baptist really saw fit to use them in this way. The derivation of the one rite from the other becomes, therefore, a matter of the similarity between them and of the ability of the supposed prototype to account for the statements about the significance of the derivative.[5]

In proselyte baptism, as described in the Talmud, the candidate for admission to Judaism completely immerses himself in the presence of appointed witnesses, namely, two learned men who stand by his side and make sure that he understands the commandments of the Jewish Law.[6] Normally this immersion is preceded by circumcision and circumcision by an inquiry into the motives of the candidate in seeking admission to Judaism. In Judæa in the period before the destruction of the city, the ablution was followed by an act of sacrifice in the Temple. Actually, then, in the Jewish homelands there were three elements in the procedure by which a man became a convert to Judaism, namely, circumcision, ablution and sacrifice. Outside Judæa proper the act of sacrifice was naturally omitted. Under circumstances of which we have no direct knowledge, moreover, persons were admitted to the faith without either sacrifice or circumcision.[7] The effect of this was to make the ceremony of immersion, where it was considered sufficient of and by itself, *the* rite of initiation into Judaism.

For the reception of the proselyte, the written Law demands merely that he be circumcised. Ablution and sacrifice are additions to the requirements of the Law, and as such are themselves in need of explanation. So far as the ablution is concerned, the probability is that it developed from the *tebilah,* a ritual bath prescribed for lay people under a variety of circumstances and for the high priest under special circumstances, to remove levitical impurity. The candidate for admission to Judaism, not having observed laws of ritual purity as a pagan, might well be expected to perform such a rite upon admission.[8] Basically, then, the rite was purificatory, but in becoming a part of the initiatory ceremony, the ablution took on new overtones. These overtones are expressed in the oft-quoted rabbinical dictum that one who has become a proselyte is like a child newly-born. When the rabbis say that the proselyte is like a newly-born child, they do not mean that a new substance has come into him from without by virtue of which he has become a new creature or has been reborn, in the sense applied to Christian baptism. The rabbis do affirm, however, that the convert with his initiation has severed his relations to a sinful past and entered upon a new state or condition of existence. That the bath itself accomplished this severance, no Jew would have declared, and that his past sins had been forgiven in connection with the event, some believed and some doubted.[9] But that a conscious dissociation from a sinful past and entrance into a condition of acceptability before God were implied in the transition, all would have agreed. These changes, which incidentally could be associated either with proselyte baptism or with circumcision, gave to the initiatory rite a connotation far beyond that of the ritual *tebilah* from which proselyte baptism had developed.

Once this is recognized the suggestion that John's baptism had proselyte ablution as its origin and inspiration reveals itself as worthy of serious consideration. Both are associated with a process of moral transformation and with personal self-dedication to God. This much is clear. Yet the differences between the two must not be overlooked. Though like proselyte ablution John's baptism occurs but once in the life of an individual, it differs in three important particulars—in being performed in running water, in having an eschatological setting, and in applying to those who are themselves already Jews. If proselyte baptism is to be taken as the source of John's rite, an account of its adaptation to Baptist purposes must be offered that will explain the differences between them.

Among the three differences listed, the most important is, undoubtedly, the fact that proselyte ablution is applied to Gentiles when they become Jews, whereas John's baptism is demanded of people who are already Jews. Of the development of this difference, two explanations have been offered. The first is that of Leipoldt, who maintains that in applying proselyte baptism to the house of Israel,

John meant to say that the entire nation had gone astray and that it needed to be reconstituted as the people of God in a new and wider sense by submitting to reinitiation on equal terms with the Gentiles.[10] In support of this interpretation he points to the saying in which John warns against relying on Abrahamic descent (Mt 3:8) and mentions God's raising up new children to Abraham from the stones of the countryside (Lk 3:8). With this saying, we have already dealt in an earlier context. If our interpretation of it is correct, it does not imply that Abrahamic descent is of no significance, but rather that to be significant, Abrahamic sonship must express itself in Abrahamic acts of exemplary piety. We found it impossible, under the circumstances, to read into the saying the thought of the rejection of Israel, and would need to protest here that there is a difference between the thought of God *being able* to raise new sons to Abraham from the stones, and the thought that he has begun to do so by creating a new community into which Jews and Gentiles come on an equal footing. As a matter of fact, the use of proselyte ablution to establish a new covenant community would be quite unlikely because, as rabbinical theology clearly states, the proselyte does not become a son of Abraham by virtue of his initiation and does not share in the merits of Abraham's exemplary life.[11] He remains on this score a step below those who are Jews by race.

A more interesting suggestion to explain how proselyte ablution could have become Baptist baptism is made

by Joachim Jeremias. He begins with a rabbinical interpretation of the reason for the use of proselyte ablution.
Several rabbis, it appears, accounted for the use of the
proselyte rite by saying that it served to put the Jew and
the new initiate on an equal footing in their religious
experience. The Jews, they declare, were baptized in the
course of the Exodus and the wilderness wandering,
whether by their passage through the Red Sea or by the
cloud that followed them, quite as Paul suggested in I
Corinthians 10. Proselyte ablution was the rite by which
Gentile initiates were made to share this experience. Now
the wilderness baptism of the Jews, Jeremias contends,
was a part of their experience of divine deliverance, deliverance from the bondage of Egypt. The eschatological
crisis which John's preaching proclaimed was to bring
with it the final deliverance of the People of God. Hence,
John instituted a new wilderness baptism analogous to
proselyte baptism, which all those could be required to
undergo who hoped to share in the world to come as their
forebears had shared in the Land of Promise.[12]

This is perhaps the most interesting explanation of
John's rite that we have had in recent years. It has its
premises in Jewish ways of thinking, copes with the eschatological and the geographical setting of John's baptism, and above all, interprets its application to the
Chosen People itself. Yet it is not without certain draw-
backs. Perhaps the most patent of these is the tendency
to attribute too high a degree of significance to the rabbinical interpretation of the passage through the Red

Sea as a wilderness baptism. Anyone who has read widely in midrashic Jewish literature will realize that every element of the Exodus narrative has been made the subject of homiletic treatment by the rabbis at some time in the course of their effort to make the record of the past illumine the life of the present. For homiletic purposes the rabbis can use the passage through the Red Sea to explain why ablution without circumcision is sufficient to make a Gentile a proselyte quite as well as Paul can use it in constructing precedents for Christian baptism (I Cor 10:1-2).[13] But whether such homiletical combinations would have had sufficient weight to suggest the institution by John of a new eschatological counterpart of the ancient wilderness experience is at least doubtful. Typological exegesis serves to explain the present but is not normally a factor in reconstituting the present. That would be putting the cart before the horse. Indeed, anyone adopting this procedure might be led to conclude that Israel, having been baptized in the wilderness, did not need to undergo a repetition of the event. Only if John felt himself called upon to create a new Israel, a new People of God, would the thought of a renewal of wilderness baptism be appropriate. For this, however, we have found no support in our interpretation of his message. What is more, John's baptism is not really described accurately as a "wilderness baptism." True, the action took place in the open, but that was because it was a baptism in running water, and neither the supposed allusion to the passage of the Red Sea, nor the analogy of proselyte baptism performed in a basin serves to explain the need for the use of running water.[14]

Failing to find in the initiatory aspects of Christian and Jewish rites a sufficient basis for the explanation of the baptism of John, some scholars fall back upon the alternative line of thought, the one suggested by the Christian conception of baptism as participation in the redemptive or regenerative process. Here antecedents in Judaism proper are naturally wanting, and those who follow this explanation have, therefore, to suppose that John was influenced by the religious thought and practice of the contemporary non-Jewish world. In recent times two monumental efforts have been made to interpret the origin of John's baptism along these lines, the first being that of R. Reitzenstein in his work *Die Vorgeschichte der christlichen Taufe* (1929), the second that of J. Thomas, *Le Mouvement Baptiste en Palestine et Syrie* (1935). Both seek to develop the thesis that acts of immersion were common features in Oriental religious observance generally in the period to which John belonged, and that in introducing such a rite into Judaism, John was changing radically the traditional Jewish conception of soteriology and the soteriological process. What caused so many rites of immersion to appear in the Orient at this time, according to Reitzenstein, was the spread of the Iranian myth that is ultimately responsible for the emergence of all redemptive religion in the ancient Græco-Roman world. The myth concerns a pre-existent heavenly being who lost some elements of his person in the cosmogonal process, elements subsequently incorporated in human beings as their souls. These elements the heavenly man seeks to recover in the course of the history of the world, thereby giving history its soteriological character. One of the instruments for the redemption of human souls in religions affected by this myth is a rite of immersion in running water, accompanied by the recital of hymns and prayers, an act of unction and participation in a sacred meal. The rite cleanses men of sin, symbolizes their reunion with deity and their return to their heavenly home. Baptism, then, as practiced in terms of this myth, is a sacrament, in part a sacrament of initiation but more particularly a sacrament of salvation and rebirth. John, we are told, adopted baptism in this sense and became thereby the medium for its transition into Christianity where its initiatory and regenerative character are more fully reflected.

To effect the connection between John the Baptist and this ultimately Iranian form of pagan redemptive religion, Reitzenstein falls back upon a baptist sect of the Orient known as the Mandeans.[15] The sect is still alive today in Mesopotamia, and has an extensive and ancient religious literature. It claims to perpetuate the movement begun by John the Baptist, and attributes to John the institution of its own baptismal rite. These claims Reitzenstein was inclined to allow, partly because of the anti-Christian and anti-Jewish orientation of the sect, partly because of its extensive traditions about John, and partly because he believed that the myth of the heavenly man which plays a prominent role in Mandean theology and soteriology was already received into Judaism by the writer of the book of Daniel, and is reflected in the figure of the Son of Man who comes on the clouds to judgment. All this being so, Mandean baptism becomes in Reitzenstein's opinion a source for our knowledge of John's baptism, and clarifies the significance of the latter as a sacrament of purification and regeneration, the precursor in this respect of Christian baptism.

What we have before us in the suggestion of Reitzenstein is another of those finely-spun, all-inclusive hypotheses that have characterized the work of the German *religionsgeschichtliche Schule*. Superior in every respect to earlier theories deriving John's baptism from Essene lustrations and associating its further development with the influence of the Mystery Religions, the hypothesis will in all probability be remembered as a testimony to the brilliance and the synthetic ability of its originator's mind rather than as an accurate account of the historical development. Whatever be true about the cosmogonal myth of the heavenly man and its reappearance in Daniel 7, it is clear that originally this myth had no cultic and soteriological associations, and hence no connection with a rite of ablution. Moreover, at no point in the long history of what may properly be called Iranian religious belief and observance is there satisfactory evidence for the use of a rite of ablution that had sacramental significance. This is by all odds the weakest point of the whole hypothesis.[16]

So far as Mandaic baptism is concerned, we shall probably have to regard it as a separate element of the Mandaic synthesis, a factor by the adoption of which it became possible to extend a theogonal and cosmogonal myth into the soteriological sphere of thought and thus to produce a Gnostic system. From whatever source the Mandeans may have derived their baptism, the probability is that its significance as they understand it is a product of the religious syncretism of the later Roman Orient. This means that we cannot use the Mandaic rite as a key to the interpretation of the Baptist-Christian development, and none of the evidence for the use of other lustrative practices in Syria and Palestine collected by Thomas in his erudite work is sufficient to show the existence of anything equally specific that might serve in its stead. What is to be done with the extensive tradition about John the Baptist himself as we meet it in the Mandaic literature, will concern us in a later context.[17]

The failure of both proselyte ablution and the Mandaic rite to provide a wholly acceptable source for the derivation of John's baptism suggests not that we should look even farther afield or return to the much abused Essenes or the Mystery Cults, but rather that we should allow for a good deal of originality and invention in its production. It should be evident from what we have seen of his life and his preaching that John was not in any sense an imitator. Rather he was a spontaneous, forceful, original personality. The fact that John could be called the Baptizer, and that Jesus could raise the question whether John's baptism was humanly or divinely authorized seems to indicate that John's originality was not limited to the sphere of his person and message but extended also—and in particular—to the rite he performed. Indeed, to assume that in its own environment it was something relatively new is precisely what we need to explain the influence it undoubtedly had not only upon the Christian Church but also upon syncretistic circles in the century that followed.

To say that we would do well to allow for a goodly measure of originality in John's baptism does not mean that it was created in a vacuum, out of nothing at all. Invention always involves the presence of environmental factors related to the new development. The point is, rather, that we should regard these factors as suggestive and not as definitive of the inauguration and the meaning of the rite. Suggestions for the development of John's baptism contemporary Judaism itself may well be said to offer, and to understand them for what they are we must call attention to a basic premise of baptismal usage, namely this, that water bathing can and does have religious significance.

The religious significance of the use of water is something that can be traced back through millennia of history in the life of the ancient Orient. Among Orientals the Semite in particular was inclined to regard water as a sacred element and, therefore, to ascribe to it healing and purifying powers.[18] In the earliest phases of their development the Hebrews apparently made only scant use of lustrations in religious practice, and in the pre-exilic period of their residence in Palestine they seem to have limited the use of religious ablutions to those directly associated with the deity or the cult, or to unusual persons or places. In the post-exilic period, however, lustrative practices were greatly extended and made obligatory for priests and laymen alike under a great variety of circumstances. The Priestly Code reflects these later developments most clearly and specifies ablutions both of the members and of the body as a whole for different types of people, making them henceforth familiar factors in the religious life of all Palestinian Jews.[19]

It is clear that in the period which saw the rise of the Pharisaic, the Baptist and the Christian movements there was a pronounced tendency to extend the use of lustrative washings even beyond the scope of the prescriptions laid down in the Priestly Code. In part this extension comes to expression in interpretations of the Code itself, for instance in the interpretation which raises to five the number of immersions and to ten the number of hand and foot ablutions that the High Priest was obliged to perform on the Day of Atonement.[20] In part it reveals itself in new supplementary and extra-legal ablutions practised by those seeking a higher piety. One of these supplements, the washing of the hands before the regular morning prayer, is attested as early as the Letter of Aristeas (§§ 304–306). Another, the washing of hands before meals, is the occasion of a dispute between Jesus and the Pharisees (Mk 7:3–4).

111

The interesting thing about this tendency is the fact that eventually it creates inside the Jewish religious community special groups set off from the rest in large measure, it would seem, by their lustrative rites. The most innocuous of the groups is that of the "morning bathers," who carry their fear of levitical impurity so far as to bathe rather than merely to wash the hands before morning prayer. Related to them but perhaps not identical with them are the Hemerobaptists of whom the Christian Apologists speak. Among the Hemerobaptists a daily ritual bath seems to have been a regular religious requirement. How early such groups came into existence is not known. The evidence about them belongs to the middle of the second century A.D. For the earlier period we have only individuals like the anchorite Bannus and groups like the Essenes to point to. Bannus, with whom Josephus spent three years in the wilderness, owes his reputation as a man of outstanding piety in no small measure to his frequent washings by night and day, and the Essenes, whatever the ultimate basis of their sectarianism, also practised lustrations in excess of traditional Jewish requirements, performing a ritual bath before each midday meal and distinguishing between the purificatory value either of different types of water or of different types of washings.[21]

No one of the practices referred to, and no combination of any number of them, provide a direct source for the baptism of John. In bulk, however, they indicate that in the anxious search for acceptability before God, groups and individuals in later Judaism turned to ablutions as a factor of some importance for the achievement of their end. It is this tendency to find in lustration an important instrument of religious usage that may account, in part at least, for the rabbis' willingness to regard proselyte ablution as sufficient for admission to Judaism, without the addition of circumcision. Indeed, in the light of this tendency we may be justified in saying that if, at the beginning of our era, a new rite was to be inaugurated among the Jews and was to achieve for itself the popularity of John's baptism, that rite would in all probability be a rite of washing. Immersion being the most radical form of ablutionary procedure, the chances are that such a new rite created in this setting would involve a full bath and thus be of the type of baptism.

Save for proselyte ablution, all of the washings in excess of the requirement of the Law with which we have dealt are ritually lustrative in character and have to be repeated from day to day. This indicates that, if we are to explain the origin and significance of John's baptism in an environment devoted to the religious use of water, we must look for some special circumstance that will give the act of immersion a higher religious meaning, making it in some sense a crucial, climactic experience in the religious life of the individual. To be relevant, this circumstance must at the same time explain why it is that for John's rite running water is necessary.

Now the one circumstance that distinguishes John's baptism from all the other ablutionary rites of later Judaism is its eschatological context, its association with a proclamation of the coming day of judgment. This, it would seem, is the sphere within which we must look for the key to the peculiar climactic significance of the rite, as Schweitzer has already suggested.[22] Among the eschatological sayings of the Baptist we have one—the saying contrasting baptism with water and baptism with Spirit and fire—that may help us to suggest a possible setting for the inauguration of the rite.

The eschatological implications of the saying about the two baptisms we have already developed in a previous context. In its original import, the saying seemed to imply that the messianic judge would destroy the wicked with his fiery breath.[23] We found the counterpart of this in the statement of II Thessalonians 2:8 that the Lord Jesus will slay the Lawless One with the breath of his mouth. What we did not try to explain in the previous context was why the destruction of the wicked by the fiery breath of the Messiah should be called a baptism, and what the force of comparison between this second baptism and the water baptism of John might be said to be. To develop the significance of the utterance further along these lines it is important to realize first that the metaphor of the fiery breath is only one of several that describe the judgment, and second, that behind these changing metaphors stands a very vivid, concrete conception of the procedure of that judgment.

The first of these points can be clarified without difficulty by a glance at the metaphors of the Book of

Revelation. In Revelation 11:5 we hear about the two witnesses whom God has sent to Jerusalem that if any man desires to hurt them, fire proceeds out of their mouths and devours their enemies. In Revelation 19:15, in the description of the warrior Messiah who rides on the white horse, the fiery breath is replaced by a sharp sword that proceeds from the Messiah's mouth with which he also destroys his enemies. The sword proceeding from the Messiah's mouth is naturally another way of describing the fiery breath in the ever-changing pattern of eschatological imagery.

The second of the two points requires for its clarification a fuller acquaintance with the role of fire in the process of judgment.[24] In the earlier period of prophecy the allusions to fire in the description of judgment are entirely metaphorical, judgment being described as like a refiner's fire or like a fiery oven (Mal 3:2; 4:1). Later, however, the fire of judgment changes from a metaphor to a reality and in the Book of Enoch we hear about the fiery pit that is to open in the familiar Valley of Hinnom to receive the wicked. The same pit appears in the Book of Revelation as the Lake of Fire into which are cast the devil, the beast, the false prophet, death and Hades (Rev 19:20; 20:10; 21:8). This "hell-fire" was very real in first-century Judaism and its reality has been preserved through centuries in Christian religious tradition.

Older in point of time than the Lake of Fire, so far as our literary evidence goes, is another equally graphic representation of the function of fire in the process of judg-

ment. It appears for the first time in Daniel 7:10 where
we read about a fiery stream that comes forth from before
the Ancient of Days as he sits upon his throne in judgment. This fiery stream, the river of fire, has a long history in Jewish and Christian apocalyptic that has only
recently been brought within our field of vision by the
work of Edsman.[25] The river of fire proceeds from under
the throne of the Messiah or will descend when the Son
of Man appears for judgment. In the later Christian texts
it has only a minor function to fulfill. So in his *24th
Homily* on Luke 3:16, in which he discusses the word of
John about baptism with Holy Spirit and with fire, Origen
says that Christians who have been baptized with water
and Spirit but lack purification are baptized after death
by Christ in the river of fire and are thereby enabled to
enter paradise. Here baptism with Spirit is distinguished
from baptism with fire and the fire baptism is reduced to
a supplementary, purificatory role. But Origen still has
the proper associations for the interpretation of the passage on which he is commenting. He knows that baptism
with fire refers not to Pentecost but to an act of judgment
on the part of the Messiah, whether it was executed by
the Messiah's fiery breath or by the river of fire proceeding out from under the throne of the judge. Originally,
it is clear, judgment executed by the river of fire involved
particularly the unrighteous, for in later Jewish apocrypha and haggadah we hear that the stream of fire that
flows from the throne falls upon the heads of the wicked
in Gehenna, or as in IV Ezra (13:10–11) destroys the

enemies of the Son of Man, while in Daniel (7:10–11) it serves as the medium for the destruction of the beast.

Even before the full significance of the river of fire in apocalyptic thought was developed by Edsman, historians of later Jewish religion had pointed to ancient Iranian conceptions reflected in the pahlavi *Bundahišn* as analogies to the judicial function of the fiery element. In Persian eschatology, the mountains which are made of metal melt at the end of the world, and the molten metal pours over the earth like a river. All men pass into this river of molten metal and in so doing are either purified or destroyed. Since in Persian thought this conception, already presupposed in the Gathas, is part of a well-coordinated system of eschatology, it is entirely possible that we have here the ultimate source of all those realistic interpretations of the function of fire in the final judgment, and thus also the source of Daniel's river of fire and its variant, the fiery breath of the Messiah.[26]

If we are permitted by the word about the two baptisms to assume that this conception of judgment by a fiery torrent was a part of John's eschatological imagery, it becomes possible to suggest a basis for the inauguration by him of a rite of immersion that had eschatological associations. The suggestion is simply this, that the water of baptism represents and symbolizes the fiery torrent of judgment, and that the individual by voluntarily immersing himself in the water enacts in advance before God his willing submission to the divine judgment which the river of fire will perform. John's baptism would, therefore, be a rite symbolic of the acceptance of the judgment which he proclaimed.[27]

Starting from the assumption that in John's baptism the individual pre-enacts his judgment, those aspects of its performance that distinguish it from contemporary Jewish lustrations, and the scattered allusions to its significance that we mentioned at the outset, find a ready explanation. John's baptism had an eschatological context because it dramatized an eschatological event. John's baptism was practiced in running water because running water was necessary to the symbolism of submersion in the river of fire. John's baptism was a baptism of repentance because by his symbolic submission to the judgment of God the individual declared himself a sinner who deserved punishment at God's hand, and at the same time affirmed the sovereignty of God over him. Finally John's baptism was applicable to all, including the Jews themselves, because before the judgment seat of God all needed to repent.

John's baptism, then, may be said to have transformed the act of immersion, currently the favored medium of the search for higher purity, into a dramatization of the substance of the eschatological expectation, currently one of the most powerful elements of religious thought. In the combination of these two factors lay the secret of its success as a rite.

Only one question requires further elucidation in the present context, namely, what effect John's baptism was supposed to have upon those who accepted and performed it. The question at issue here is whether baptism as John practiced and preached it was a sacrament and, if so, in what sense. On this point also there has been a wealth of discussion, some scholars maintaining that it was a sacrament of initiation, others that it was a sacrament of the forgiveness of sins.

For the initiatory significance of John's rite, stoutly defended where proselyte baptism is regarded as its inspiration, two arguments are commonly advanced. The first is that Josephus speaks of John calling the people to "come together" in baptism, and the second that communities of Baptist disciples actually came into existence in Palestine as the result of John's preaching and baptism.[28] So far as the statement of Josephus is concerned, the expression used is much too weak to carry the thought of "uniting themselves" by baptism, as some maintain, and means only that the people were invited to come as a people must, in numbers rather than each one separately. So far as the disciples of John are concerned, two things must be kept in mind. The first is that the disciple phenomenon of later Judaism has its roots in concepts of religious authority rather than of ritual performance. The second is that even a movement which originally aspired to influence the entire Jewish people could, if it failed in its effort, have survived only in the form of a minority organization. Later developments are, therefore, no infallible clue to original intent. Actually John could have meant by baptism to constitute a new Israel only if he believed that God had rejected the Israel of old, and the word about God raising up new children to Abraham from the stones of the wilderness does not reflect this conception, if we have correctly interpreted it. True, the threat of rejection hangs over the present Israel and of its children some will assuredly not escape the divine wrath, but for John to preach repentance and to institute a baptism of repentance under these circumstances is to imply that he seeks to bring to the perfection of Abrahamic piety the sons of Abraham and not to constitute a new Chosen People. How, if baptism was not at first initiatory it could later have acquired this significance, we shall see in another context.[29]

That John's rite, even though it was not initiatory, was nonetheless a sacrament, is frequently affirmed, nowhere more bluntly than in the words of Rudolf Otto, "With John the forgiveness of sins took place through a magical, sacramental rite of washing."[30] The arguments for the sacramental interpretation of John's baptism derived from its supposed dependence upon pagan rites need not concern us here. Pagan lustrative ceremonies which worked magically did exist, particularly in the west, but no one of them can be brought within effective proximity of the time and place of the Baptist. Everything turns, therefore, upon the interpretation of the statement of Mark 1:4 that John came preaching a baptism of repentance "for the forgiveness of sins." Specifically, the question is how are the forgiveness and the baptism associated. At this point, as we have previously noted, there is an apparent contradiction between Mark

on the one side and Josephus on the other, the latter
maintaining that according to John baptism was not to
be used to beg off from sins committed.[31] In all probability the contradiction is more apparent than real. It
can be ironed out by the assumption that Mark's words,
"for the forgiveness of sins," describe not the action of
the rite itself, but the action of God associated with the
performance of the rite by man.[32] The distinction made
in this assumption is fundamental to the operation of all
ritual acts in Judaism, where the validity of rite invariably depends upon the divine command which in-
stitutes it and upon the attitude of the people performing
it. Judaism throughout the many centuries of its history
never produced a rite which was efficacious of and by
itself, hence a sacrament, and it is doubtful whether John
would have departed from the Jewish point of view in
this particular. In fact it would seem that the whole
point of Josephus' comment about what John's baptism
did not do, was to make it clear to his pagan readers that,
whatever the outward similarity to magically operative
rites familiar to them, there was no sacramentalism in
anything properly Jewish. How, if John's baptism was
not sacramental, it could still be associated with the forgiveness of sin as Mark says, is easy to understand. The
reason is that as an act of self-humiliation before God
it was a clear, voluntary expression of true repentance,
and that repentance was commonly acknowledged to have
divine forgiveness as its response. If John's baptism, then,
was an act of repentance it could mediate forgiveness

without conferring it. It could mediate forgiveness without being a sacrament.

If we are right in assuming that as a symbolic act expressing repentant submission to God's judgment the baptism of John was an innovation in the field of religious rite, its importance in John's own life-time and in the religious developments of the first two centuries of our era, Christian and syncretistic alike, becomes relatively clear. For centuries the eschatological sphere of Jewish religious thought had been growing in importance. It needed a rite in which its essential hopes and fears could be brought to expression and in connection with which its burdens could be lifted from the human mind. John's baptism supplied that rite, and with what force we can imagine if we realize that it called upon men to place themselves now, in the present, before the judgment throne and to understand that only by the act of repentant submission now could they hope to escape from the terrors of a future immersion, immersion in the fiery torrent of judgment in the day that was to come.

V

John the Baptist and Jesus

NO discussion of John the Baptist would be complete without full consideration of the relation between him and Jesus of Nazareth. In part this is because John's impact upon his contemporaries is nowhere more strikingly illustrated than in the case of Jesus. In part it is because Jesus and the Christian Church profoundly affected the further development of the Baptist movement, being at one and the same time the occasion for its transformation and disintegration and the instrument for the perpetuation of its memory and its rite. Yet no aspect of the life and work of John is more difficult to describe and interpret correctly than that of his relation to Jesus. The reason is, of course, that our information about it comes exclusively from Christian observers and that to them the connection between the two men was a source both of joy and embarrassment.

The early Christians knew of the personal contact

123

between Jesus and John and of the words that Jesus had spoken about John according him a high place in the divine order of salvation. This information they transmitted gladly not only because of the prominence of John in their day and generation but also because of the conviction that Jesus and John really belonged together. Yet their faith in Jesus as Christ and Lord demanded that they avoid imputing to another anything even suggesting the possibility of equal dignity and importance, and the conflict in which they were early embroiled with the staunchest adherents of the Baptist on this score apparently caused them to qualify their reports on the relation between the two men. Seizing upon the word of John about the Coming One, in which they inevitably saw a prophecy of the coming of Jesus himself, they devolved a formula for the interpretation of the relationship that satisfied the demands of their faith and has become a classic in the Christian interpretation of the Baptist. John was, they said, the divinely appointed Forerunner of Jesus, not only in his anticipated function as messianic judge but in his human manifestation. The course of history has given substance to their interpretation, but it remains a value-judgment and in this capacity has the power both to give meaning to and to distort historical fact.

For any effort to interpret correctly the relation of John and Jesus the first requirement is to understand the nature of this basic formula and to assign it to its proper place. The second requirement is to make the proper

allowance for the qualifying factors that Christian thinking and the Christian faith have introduced into the
record of the relation between the two men and to establish a residuum of inescapable fact. In this connection it
is necessary to determine the issues that were in dispute
between Baptist and Christian sympathizers as set forth
in the following chapter, for only this knowledge provides
the proper understanding of the points at which allowance must be made. The third requirement is to take the
residuum of inescapable fact and to give it its proper
place in a possible historical development. We shall endeavor to apply these procedures and principles to the
two types of material at our disposal, namely, the relevant
narratives and sayings of the Gospels. The sayings are
much the easier to handle, but the discussion must begin
with the narratives and must come back to them after
the sayings have been brought into the picture.

Our narrative material contains reports of a whole
series of encounters between John the Baptist and Jesus.
According to one of the latest strands of Gospel tradition
the two were brought together even before they were
born. After the Annunciation, so Luke tells us, the youth-
ful Mary visited the aged Elisabeth, already great with
child, and at her salutation the unborn John "leaped" in
Elisabeth's womb in joyous recognition of his great Successor's advent, causing his mother to call Mary and her
child blessed (Lk 1:39–56). We have already had occasion to see that the episode serves as the medium that
ties the Baptist Infancy Narrative and the Christian

Nativity Story together.[1] In the present context it is important to note the bearing of the narrative upon the controversy between Christian and Baptist groups. In effect, the story undercuts all claims to the autonomous importance of the Baptist by showing that both he and his mother recognized Jesus as the greater at the outset. This recognition communicated by the details of the narrative itself is stated also in so many words by Elisabeth when she comments on the amazing fact that the "mother of her Lord" should deign to visit her (Lk 1:43). What is more, the story, based on the assumption that Mary and Elisabeth are blood relatives (Lk 1:36), endows Jesus from his mother's side with any advantages of Aaronic descent that John could boast, making him, as a descendant both of David and of Aaron, the inevitable choice among those through whom the national hope of deliverance might be thought to come to fulfillment. Anyone keeping these facts in mind will find it hard to escape the conclusion that the story is a product of the struggle between Christian and Baptist loyalties, an effort of the Christian disciples to show the superiority of their Master. Yet this does not deprive it of all evidential value, for behind the story is the perfectly valid fundamental assumption that John and Jesus stand in relation to each other. What has happened in this case, as so often in popular religious tradition, is that a personal relation between two people, known to be an important historical fact, is projected back into their own antecedents on the assumption that this will prevent the relationship from being misinterpreted as fortuitous and incidental. Seen in this light, the story is a testimony to an important Christian conviction and a conviction that is fundamentally sound, for certainly what brought Jesus and John together was not coincidence. It is only the fact that the ancients commonly stated such conviction in story form and that in this instance the story reflects the controversy in which the Christian believers were engaged that tends to obscure for some its character and significance.

Elsewhere in Gospel record John and Jesus come into contact with each other only as adults and this at four separate occasions, namely, at the baptism of Jesus (Mk 1:9–11 and parallels), when John saw Jesus "coming" (Jn 1:29) and "walking" (Jn 1:36) and when John sent a delegation of his disciples to Jesus (Mt 11:2–6 = Lk 7:19–23). The three episodes that belong to the period after Jesus' baptism present difficulties. So far as concerns the two reported solely by the Fourth Evangelist, they are little more than occasions for John to give his witness to Jesus as the Lamb of God and thereby to encourage his disciples to transfer their allegiance from himself to Jesus. Scholarship has always had difficulty reconciling these encounters and their witness with the Synoptic account of the delegation sent by John from prison to ask Jesus, "Art thou he that cometh?" (Mt 11:3; Lk 7:20) and in fact they are in absolute conflict. Yet the fact of their being in conflict tells us less about them than does the christological conception with which they operate and the potential value which they have as instruments of anti-Baptist polemic. As regards the former, it should be evident that there is no way of reconciling what is implied in the term Lamb of God with what John's own words as recorded in the earlier Gospels tell us about his conception of the messianic judge and the way of salvation. As regards the latter, it should be clear that for John personally to instruct his disciples about Jesus' pre-existence, the function of the descent of the Spirit at Jesus' baptism and about the atoning value of Jesus' death, is not only to discourage them henceforth from attributing to himself any value whatsoever, but also to encourage them to adopt that formulation of the Christian faith that was current at an advanced period in the history of the early Church. Again, therefore, the historicity of the reported encounters is questionable, the importance of the stories for us being rather to highlight an ancient conviction that the meeting of the two men was not fortuitous but continuous, having a profound significance for them both, and that had John lived to witness the later events in the life of Jesus and of the early Church he would have given his personal allegiance to the new Christian faith. Whether all parts of this conviction are equally valid is a question to which we will return later.

The account of the delegation sent by the imprisoned John to Jesus, as reported in our Second Source and rendered by Matthew and Luke is equally difficult, though for quite other reasons. It belongs to a period and an environment entirely different from that of the Fourth

Evangelist, judged by its presuppositions and by the issues to which it seems to address itself. It concurs in Mark's testimony that John spent no small amount of time in prison (Mk 6:20), knows that Jesus began preaching after John had been incarcerated (Mk 1:14) and that the preaching was accompanied by "signs and wonders" as all three Synoptic Evangelists clearly point out. In other words, the story is well informed judging by the evidence available to us. What it purports to do with this information is to settle a christological problem, namely, that of the identity of the Coming One, which is why the delegation of John's disciples asks Jesus, "Art thou he?"

So far as John himself is concerned, the problem is completely unreal if his words about the messianic judge are fully trustworthy and have been correctly interpreted. There is for John no possible meeting-ground between the wonder-working preacher of the Kingdom and the transcendent "man-like one" who destroys the wicked in unquenchable fire, save on the assumption of a break with his fundamental convictions, for which there is no adequate justification. Nor can the problem have been very real to those Christians who belonged to the second generation of the early Church. For them, Jesus had already become so thoroughly familiar in his two states of humiliation and exaltation respectively that they must have found no difficulty in applying John's terminology and ideas to the Christ who returns on the clouds in judgment. Their handling of the Baptist's saying about the Mightier One who comes after him is a witness to this fact. Where the problem was acute was clearly among those who had the Baptist's proclamation still ringing in their ears, who lived in close contact with faithful disciples of John and whose thinking about Jesus was conditioned in large measure by their recollection of his life in their midst. These were the same folk who, according to Luke-Acts, proclaimed Jesus as a man approved of God by mighty works and signs and wonders (Acts 2:22). It would be most natural for them, therefore, to resolve the contrast between John's conception of the Messiah and their own faith in Jesus by thinking of the mighty works as the incontrovertible justification of their belief, especially if they could find in Scripture anything to substantiate their position.

It is quite likely, therefore, that the John who in prison begins to doubt the adequacy of his own proclamation when he hears of Jesus' mighty works, is but a foil of their own conviction, a conviction which is substantiated in what John's delegates are instructed to report back to him. The burden of this report merely reaffirms what John already knew, going beyond it in but one particular, namely, in the allusions to the prophecies of Isaiah (Is 35:5; 61:1). More than fall back upon the record and the prophets, the Christian believer himself could not do when his faith was challenged on the strength of the Baptist's proclamation. The story, then, has all the earmarks of the early Christians' own effort to resolve the problem of faith and history, and to this extent appears to provide little evidence of historical value for our knowledge of the contacts between John and Jesus.[3] Its evidential value for the study of the Baptist is in the importance which it assigns to his proclamation as something against which Christian faith must be tested. The beatitude uttered at the close of the story over those who do not take offense at Jesus brings this to forcible expression.

For narrative material bearing on the relation between John the Baptist and Jesus we have, therefore, to fall back ultimately and solely, it would seem, upon the episode of Jesus' baptism (Mk 1:9–11; Mt 3:13–17; Lk 3:21–22). Here we are on the most solid historical ground, for only one who had himself accepted baptism at John's hands could have spoken of the Baptist as Jesus did, and no one of Jesus' followers, disturbed as they were by the conflict between their faith and that of John's adherents, would have invented an episode that seemed to subordinate their Master to John. Not only are we on solid ground in the story of the baptism; we are also on ground that is of the greatest strategic importance. Quite possibly, as the record insists, there were other occasions when the two men came into contact, but by comparison these must have been relatively insignificant so that it is more of a misfortune than a calamity that we know nothing about them. Here, however, is the encounter that is all-important and Gospel record continued to keep it so until the pre-existence doctrine began to dim the memory of crucial moments that moulded the course of Jesus' life and thought as they had that of the prophets before him.

While the episode of Jesus' baptism is necessarily the most important for our understanding of the relations of John and Jesus, the narratives are strangely uniformative, at least explicitly, when viewed from this angle. In part, this is because they are so brief. In part, it is because they are concerned with things much more important for the Christian faith, namely, with Jesus' vision of the open heavens, with the descent of the Spirit upon him and with his installation in messianic office by the voice from heaven. The Fourth Gospel, it is true, makes John a participant in and, in fact, the true beneficiary of these events (Jn 1:32–33) and the Gospel according to Matthew attributes to the Baptist so much foreknowledge of the importance of Jesus as he comes to baptism that it would be anomalous indeed were he to be excluded from participation in the events that followed. Yet our earliest Gospel, Mark, is thoroughly unambiguous in ascribing the vision of the heavens torn asunder to Jesus himself and the nature of the experience is such that there is fundamentally no basis for including John in it.[4] Hence, we are left with what is for our purposes, on the surface, at least, a most unenlightening account.

The one detail that promises most by way of enlightenment and does, in fact, help us quite a bit when seen in the right perspective, is the conversation between John and Jesus just before the baptism, as reported by Matthew (Mt 3:14–15). This is the conversation in which

John protests that Jesus should come to him to be baptized and in which Jesus replies, "Suffer it now for thus it becometh us to fulfill all righteousness."

The significance of this detail can best be understood if we compare it with another still later elaboration of the story of the baptism, namely, the one which Jerome quotes from the Gospel according to the Hebrews. In the Gospel according to the Hebrews, we are told, the reflections upon the propriety of Jesus' baptism go back to the period before Jesus had ever left Galilee. Here we read:

> Behold the mother of the Lord and his brethren said unto him: John the Baptist baptizeth unto the remission of sins; let us go and be baptized of him. But he said unto them: Wherein have I sinned that I should be baptized of him, unless peradventure this very thing that I have said (i.e. Why should I be baptized?) is a sin of ignorance?[5]

Clearly those who added this episode to the earlier record regard the rite as conferring forgiveness after the manner of the Christian sacrament and were bothered by the question why Jesus should have needed to submit to it since he was *ex hypothesi* sinless. The story adroitly has Jesus himself raise the question and give the answer. Jesus is certain of his own sinlessness, but he does not know whether he might not need baptism for some other reason than for the remission of sins. Hence he prefers to undergo the rite rather than by failing to do so commit a sin of ignorance. Clearly apocryphal, the episode is interesting and instructive as an example of how tradition grows in response to the demands of problems in the minds of the transmitters.

Seen in the light of this analogy the meaning of the incident in Matthew becomes thoroughly clear. The circles which Matthew's tradition represents were not concerned over Jesus' sinlessness but over the issue of the greater being baptized by the less. Hence the words of John, "I have need to be baptized of thee and thou comest to me?" recalling the self-abnegation of his own mother in the presence of Mary (Lk 1:43). Now the particular conception of Jesus as the greater held by Matthew's circles included the thought that he was the teacher and example of the higher righteousness (Mt 5:20), and that he had commanded his followers to make disciples of all nations by baptizing them (Mt 28:19). Such baptism, the episode tells us, Jesus did not need, but since he required it of his followers as a part of the higher righteousness, he underwent it himself so that he might be for them the perfect example. Hence Jesus' answer to the Baptist implies that questions of propriety and impropriety cannot be allowed to interfere with his determination to exhibit in his own life the full measure of the righteousness he demands of others, righteousness here being understood as righteous or holy acts.[6]

If this is truly the meaning of the episode as narrated by Matthew it is of greater value for our knowledge of early Christian thought than for our understanding of the relation of John and Jesus. For the early Church,

Jesus was the highest example of righteousness, and properly so, but to make the thought of being an example the motive of his acceptance of baptism at John's hands is to pitch Jesus' ethical life at a level far below its recognizable standards. Normally Jesus acts out of deep inner compulsions that arise from his understanding of the divine will. That such an inner necessity played a part in his acceptance of baptism is attested by one salient fact of the record, namely, that the baptism became for Jesus the occasion of a profound experience described by the opening of the heavens, the descent of the Spirit and the sound of a celestial voice. Humanly speaking, such experiences are intelligible only where there is involved in the attitude of the one concerned a very special sense of consecration and of participation in the action at hand.

At this point we are in a position to look beneath the uniformative exterior of the baptismal narrative and to gauge for ourselves what it implies as to the relation between Jesus and John. The baptism implies, of course, that Jesus accepted John's proclamation. Like many others in Galilee, including some who later became his own disciples, Jesus was apparently led by his devotion to his people's hope and to its God-given destiny to wonder at what he heard about the new preacher in the wilderness and to make the pilgrimage to hear him directly. What he heard convinced him that John was the authorized spokesman of God. This meant that he accepted the imminence of the divine judgment and of the need for decision, repentance and Abrahamic piety. That it should also have meant for Jesus the acceptance of baptism as the seal and sign of repentance and of self-humiliation before the judgment throne of God, is not to be wondered at. To anyone who, like the author of the Gospel according to the Hebrews, is disturbed by the thought of a supposed conflict between this assumption and the dogma of Jesus' sinlessness it may be suggested that he replace the negative virtue of sinlessness in this context with the positive virtue of holiness for which there is ample justification in the record. History shows that the holiest of men have also been the ones most ready to humiliate themselves before God. To this rule Jesus was undoubtedly no exception.

For our knowledge of the relation of John and Jesus still more is to be gained from an analysis of the baptismal narrative, but first we must consider a series of four words of Jesus all of which reflect directly or indirectly his estimate of the Baptist. The first is the word with which Jesus in the Second Source answers the demand for a sign in proof of his divine commission (Mt 12:38–41 = Lk 11:29–30). In this word Jesus says "no sign shall be given except the sign of Jonah." Matthew or his circle believed that the allusion was to Jesus himself and has Jesus call attention to the analogy between the three nights which Jonah spent in the belly of the whale and the three days and nights which the Son of Man is to spend in the grave. Not found in Luke, this interpretation is clearly secondary, serving only the purposes of Christian apologetic in its efforts to find a scriptural basis for the death of the Master. This is indicated by the continuing context of the saying, as found in both Matthew and Luke, where reference is made to the Ninevites who repented while Israel did not. The reference has point only if the allusion in the sign of Jonah is to someone or something which was intended to cause repentance as Jonah did. Historically, this can only have been John the Baptist, whose stirring call to repentance we have already examined and found a fundamental feature of his proclamation.[7] When asked for a sign Jesus, therefore, pointed metaphorically to John, the preacher of repentance, saying that John was the only sign that the present generation would receive. By this word he thus confessed his own acceptance of John as a heaven-sent agent, set him in line with the prophets of Israel's past and accorded him a unique place in the divine economy of the present.

More familiar among Jesus' allusions to John are two other words also recorded in the Second Source and reproduced in Matthew 11:7–14 and Luke 7:24–30. Here, too, it would seem, allowance must be made for modifications of the original utterance of Jesus both in the circles represented by the Second Source and in those represented by the Evangelists, but the general sense of the statements is clear in any case. The first statement is contained in the words, "But wherefore went ye out (into the wilderness)? To see a prophet? Yea, I say unto you, and much more than a prophet. This is he of whom it is written, Behold I send my messenger before thy face." The second statement is contained in the words, "Verily I say unto you, Among them that are born of women there hath not arisen a greater than John the Baptist; yet he that is but little in the kingdom of heaven is greater than he."

The two sayings are highly significant as encomia of Jesus on John and must be authentic because the early Church was scarcely in a mood with respect to the Baptist to have created them itself. The best it could do, in our judgment, was so to emend the second of the two sayings as to create the antithesis between John and the "little in the kingdom of heaven" who are said to be "greater than he."[8] If the statement that the little in the kingdom are greater than John *is* actually, as we believe, a Christian addition to the second of the two words, its function is to remove from the utterance a threat to the primacy of Jesus "among those born of women," a primacy which faith made axiomatic. This sounds plausible, but the question is whether by the removal of this supposed emendation we have not placed ourselves in the embarrassing position of being unable to cope with what remains of the saying. Would Jesus really have said about John without qualification that he was the "greatest among them that are born of women"? Here a closer study of the expression may be of some help both in interpreting the word and in gaining support for the hypothesis that it *was* emended by the Christian community.

138

Actually, of course, Jesus does not say that John was "the greatest among those born of women." What he does say is that "there hath not arisen among those born of women a greater than John." The difference between the two formulations seems so slight at first as to be worthless, but a study of the parallels in later Jewish literature indicates that it is real nonetheless. In a single passage in the *Mehilta,* for instance, we have statements about both Joseph and Moses which use the same expression. About Joseph it is said, "there is not among his brethren one greater than he," and about Moses "there is not in Israel one greater than he."[9] As used in Jewish texts such statements are not to be taken as blanket judgments; they are made apropos of a specific trait of the individual in question in respect to which he is outstanding. So in the passage of the *Mehilta* under discussion there is no one among Joseph's brethren greater than he in respect to the piety which he exhibited in journeying to Palestine to bury his father Jacob, and there is no one greater in Israel than Moses in respect to his piety in bringing with him from Egypt the bones of Joseph.

The analogies from later Jewish literature suggest that in speaking of John as one of whom there was not a greater, Jesus also had some specific quality or function of the Baptist in mind to which this traditional formula could be applied. Only a later generation which did not understand the formula and did not recall the specific trait that it commended saw in the saying a threat to Jesus' primacy and, therefore, emended it by the addition of the words about the "little in the kingdom." If the emendation is thus made intelligible, what shall we say about the original burden of the encomium? Here we can only conjecture, but the context suggests that it was John's function as a prophet that was originally in Jesus' mind. The saying would then mean that among the children of men there had never arisen a greater prophet than was John. So interpreted the word takes us beyond the statement implying that John was second Jonah, but it does not tell us upon what his claim to equality with the greatest actually rests. At this point Jesus' answer to the rhetorical question "Wherefore went you out (into the wilderness)? To see a prophet?" can help us further.

To understand the answer which Jesus gives to this question we must recall that in the last century of Jewish national existence there were apparently many who claimed to be prophets or were so regarded by certain sections of the people. The mysterious Egyptian, with whom Paul was confused (Acts 21:38), and the Theudas mentioned by Gamaliel in Acts (5:36) were men of this type. As Josephus describes them they claimed to be prophets and gathered large groups of followers in the wilderness, promising that signs would not be lacking to accredit them as spokesmen of God.[10] In the language of the Gospels such men are "false prophets" and "false messiahs" who would lead the people astray. Under these circumstances, if Jesus, having set aside as nonsensical

the thought of going out into the wilderness to see a reed
or a man in soft rainment, suggests that such a journey
implies the presence in the wilderness of a prophet, he
has not yet affirmed more than that men of such repute
drew crowds into the desert whether or not their claims
to prophetic authority were justified. Hence, when Jesus
goes on to say, "Yes, and more than a prophet," his words
serve not to remove the Baptist from the prophetic category entirely but to indicate that he was more than other
"would-be" prophets of the wilderness; he was indeed
a "true" prophet. But according to the context, at least,
the "more" has still further connotations. John can be
said to be "more," a "true" prophet, because he is the
one of whom it is written, "Behold I send my messenger
before thy face." That is, John is Elijah returned to
prepare the way for the coming of the Lord. Here the
analogy to Jonah is given up and John's equality with
the greatest of the prophets is explained in terms of
his unique relation to the fulfillment of the eschatological
hope.

The suggestion that John was Elijah returned to fulfill his eschatological role is one that we find reflected
in many parts of Gospel record. In at least three instances, namely, in the passage before us, in the opening
verses of Mark and in the *Benedictus* of the birth story,
the suggestion turns on the use of the familiar passage
Malachi 3:1. To these we must add the enigmatic conversation between Jesus and his disciples after the Trans-
figuration as reported in Mark 9:9–13, where two unre-

lated elements of the tradition are apparently combined unsuccessfully. Both elements concern the proximity of the coming of the Kingdom of God. The first involves the question of the disciples, "Must not Elijah come first," to which Jesus answers by saying "Elijah does come" and again "Elijah has come." The second involves the unspoken query, "Then why is the Kingdom not already here?" to which Jesus responds with the question, "How is it written about the Son of Man that he should suffer and be set at naught," the implication being that the Kingdom comes only after the Passion and Resurrection. From the combination of the two the inference is apparently to be drawn that, if the Son of Man has to be set at naught, the same might well hold true of Elijah, in which case John could well have been Elijah in spite of his ignominious end. All details here are quite obscure, but at least this is clear; that John's identity as Elijah returned is being upheld even in the face of his death at the hands of Herod Antipas.[11] The same confident assurance is reflected in the statement which Matthew adds to the passage from the Second Source that served as our starting point, namely, the statement about John, "If you are willing to receive it, this is Elijah that is to come. He that hath ears to hear let him hear."

Not all of these testimonies are equally impressive as first-hand evidence, but their cumulative force can scarcely be denied, especially in view of the pains which the Fourth Evangelist takes to make John deny that he is Elijah (Jn 1:21). As a matter of fact, there were many

things about John that suggested his identification with
Elijah, his preaching of the imminent judgment, the
austerity of his life and conduct, his dress, his sojourn
in the wilderness, his activity in the very area from which
Elijah had, according to the Old Testament, been taken
up into heaven, his bold opposition to Antipas and his
intense devotion to the welfare of his nation. There is
no reason why these facts so evident to all and so meaningful to others should not have been equally suggestive
to Jesus. The only question is whether what Jesus thought
on this score can be combined with the statements that
John was a second Jonah and that he was without peer
among prophets.

Perhaps the word quoted by Matthew (11:14-15),
namely, "If you are willing to receive it this is Elijah that
is to come; He that hath ears to hear, let him hear," can
help us at this point. As others have already pointed out
the clauses with which the central affirmation is hedged
about, to wit, "If you are willing to receive it" and "He
that hath ears to hear, let him hear," are characteristic
of utterances that belong to the category of the mysterious and the esoteric.[12] Something is being said with
their help which is not evident to all and which requires
on the part of the hearer some desire and ability to probe
the deeper recesses of insight and meaning. That Jesus
did not make a cult of the mysterious is evident from
the unaffected simplicity of the majority of his words.
Equally evident, however, is the fact that he had and
brought to expression in his words flashes of insight, the

carrying power of which he was himself, perhaps, only dimly aware at the moment. The words about those who should not taste death till they should see the Kingdom coming with power, about casting out demons by the finger of God, and about Satan falling from heaven belong to this category. It is basically probable that the words associating John with Elijah are of the same type, in which case they would have both the value and the limitations of intuitive judgments. So interpreted, the words would not in any sense conflict with the analogous statements suggesting that John was a second Jonah and equal to the greatest of the prophets. In fact, the variety of allusion, moving in the single category of the prophetic, does more to confirm the historical value of the material than would a single parroted stereotype.

What our study of his sayings has taught us about Jesus' opinion of John underscores heavily the impression gleaned from the account of Jesus' baptism. After all, it is not just anybody whom Jesus would have called a true prophet, much less a prophet without peer, still less Elijah. His own religious life and thought were too deeply rooted in the prophetic tradition of his people for that. Rather, from what we know of Jesus' own religious thought we should have to conclude that for him prophecy was a sacred thing, a gift of God to men, something that lifted them above themselves and made them instruments of divine purpose. Hence, for Jesus to call John a prophet was more than a mark of respect. It implied that, confronted with John's preachment, he found himself in the presence of the divine revelation and bowed in gratitude to the God who had given such revelation to men. But there is more here even than this. Later Judaism believed that since the days of Malachi the voice of prophecy had been divinely stilled and the gift withdrawn.[13] So when the Maccabeans lacked a prophet to tell them what to do with the stones of the altar that Antiochus IV had profaned, they merely rolled them to one side till prophecy should be reborn through the return of Elijah.[14] For Jesus to affirm that in John prophecy *had* been reborn, therefore, meant more than that another name was to be added to the list of the great. It meant that now the last days were at hand, as John had said, and that John was the one sent by Heaven to prepare the way. These affirmations so often made by Jesus must have their basis in deep impressions created during direct personal contact with the Baptist. Properly understood, the relevant words of Jesus and the narrative of Jesus' baptism by John are in fundamental accord in what they tell us of the impact of the Baptist upon his greater contemporary.

It would be of great value to us if we could see also the reverse side of the coin and know what impressions Jesus made on John. Unfortunately, this seems impossible. The eloquent testimonies of John to Jesus in the Fourth Gospel and the query of the Second Source, "Art thou he that cometh?" cancel each other out, as we have already seen, and they are all the evidence we have. At this point, then, the veil of history is closely drawn and

145

it is useless to try to lift it or mourn the restrictions it imposes.

If all that has been said about the significance of John for Jesus is actually in accord with the facts, one peculiarity of the life and teaching of Jesus must necessarily excite the historian's curiosity and cause him to wonder. It is this, that Jesus should have differed from John at so many salient points in his conduct and his religious thought. Here we reach the ultimate issue in the study of the relation of Jesus and John, and pose at the same time fundamental problems of the origin and nature of the distinctively Christian Gospel. The matter is well worth closer scrutiny, even for our immediate purposes.

To set forth the more important differences between Jesus and John is by no means difficult. Jesus was an itinerant preacher carrying his message from hamlet to hamlet, John a sojourner in the wilderness who expected men to come to him. John lived in the wilderness the frugal life of a nomad and imposed upon himself in addition the practice of fasting. Jesus rejected the necessity or propriety of fasting and was called by his opponents a "glutton and a wine-bibber." John practiced the rite of baptism, Jesus did not. Jesus construed the imminent eschatological event as the occasion for joy, John found it fraught with terror. John demanded exemplary conduct in the ways of righteousness, the fulfillment of all that the Law demanded and a "more" that the times required as the positive expression of a repentant life.

Jesus waived the letter of the Law and saw no virtue in observantism. John preached a righteous God who was soon to institute judgment. Jesus emphasized God's desire to seek the lost and to be merciful to the sinner. For John, the day of reckoning, though close at hand, was still to come. For Jesus, the Kingdom, while still largely future, was already in a sense present.

To list these differences is much easier than to account for them if what we have said about the significance of the Baptist for Jesus is correct. Goguel has attempted to solve the problem by suggesting a definite break at one time in Jesus' relation to John.[15] Originally, he thinks, Jesus proclaimed John's message of doom and repentance, baptized men and demanded of them a life of observance. Traces of the demands he made during this "collaborative" phase of his career are said still to be visible in the Sermon on the Mount, particularly in the requirement that men shall be perfect as their Father in heaven is perfect. Eventually, as the result of a divine revelation which made him conscious of a messianic mission, he broke with John, the break coinciding with the time of his coming into Galilee (Mk 1:14). From this time on he preached a new doctrine, the "Gospel." His followers subsequently projected the preaching of this Gospel back into the earliest days of his public career, thereby obscuring the difference between Jesus the disciple of John and Jesus the bringer of the Kingdom.

The hypothesis presented is highly suggestive and worthy of serious consideration. There is no reason to dwell here upon its incidental details and thus to argue whether John ever used the expression "Kingdom of God," to inquire whether Jesus' messianic consciousness is a necessary part of the picture, or to become embroiled in the discussion of the term Nazarene. The important thing is to understand the inferences drawn from certain aspects of Jesus' teaching and the use made in this connection of certain elements of Gospel tradition.

Goguel conceives of the break between Jesus and John as having arisen from the former's conception of the absolute transcendence of God. Seen in the light of this transcendence and absolute righteousness, he feels, all human effort, even including repentance, loses its value, for it still leaves man short of acceptability before God. When this became clear to him, Goguel believes, Jesus abandoned the program of preparing a righteous people and thus broke with the Baptist.

There can be no doubt, it would seem, that the absolute transcendence of God did play a part in Jesus' thought, and Goguel is entirely right in pointing to the word describing men as "unprofitable servants" (Lk 17:7–10) to show that negative conclusions could be and were drawn from it. But to make this facet of Jesus' thought the determining factor in his attitude toward observance, whether of John's baptism or of the Law, would appear to be unfortunate. Rather, it would seem that his attitude in these matters should be associated with his equally clear conception of God's mercy and saving will. Finding this saving will quite as radical and unconditioned as

God's righteousness, Jesus endeavors in his teaching as in his life to exhibit a human response that is given in kind. His ethical imperatives bespeak on the part of man confronted with the miracle of God's search of the sinner and with his purpose to give to men the Kingdom, a living answer to God's love quite as creative, spontaneous, and unconditional in its character and outreach as the love to which it responds. To prescribe fixed channels for it and to regard these as normative is to limit it and thus to destroy its responsive character and its creative power. Consequently even the Law cannot be used to prescribe and delimit. It serves rather to point and to stimulate, but man, to the extent that he is truly motivated by the personal experience of the divine self-revelation, will surely find meaning in the divine institutions and injunctions whether of the Law or of the Prophets or of John.

If what has been said about the nature of his teaching is correct, Jesus, too, is seeking an exemplary conduct, but he follows a different line of thought in his efforts to achieve it. There is no basis here for a break between Jesus and John over a matter of principle. Jesus merely insists that since the example is God rather than Abraham, the individual must be as free as God himself is to make his relation to God and man creatively and spontaneously meaningful. To adopt Goguel's interpretation of the break between the two men would be to imply that Jesus must have regretted ever having been baptized by John. This would reduce to a mere farce Jesus' action in posing the question, "John's baptism, was it from

149

heaven or from men?" (Mk 11:30). To follow the line of thought suggested here would be to imply that without denying the significance it had for him personally, Jesus refused to assert that baptism must have the same value for others and hence did not choose himself to perpetuate its performance even if that had been possible under the circumstances of his itinerant activity and of the area in which he felt called upon to work.

It is one thing to state objections to a given hypothesis such as Goguel's and quite another thing to put a better in its place. Until this last has at least been attempted, Jesus' relation to John cannot be regarded as having been treated adequately. In accounting for the peculiar nature of the relationship, due allowance will, of course, have to be made for the tendency of environment and of differences in personality to assert themselves in conditioning the divergent points of view of the two men. Coming from a rural priestly family of Judæa, John, with his more impulsive temperament, responded naturally to the contradiction between the traditional ideals of his caste and the secularization of the urban priesthood with invective and with threats of divine punishment. Jesus, on the other hand, brought up as one of the "quiet in the land" among the religiously starved and suspect "poor" of Galilee, reacted to the unfortunate lot of his countrymen with a simple message of comfort and uplift.

Modern criticism and historiography will naturally make use gratefully of all that a study of background and personality can contribute to our interpretation of the differences between two or more persons. But important as these factors are, they are usually not enough. Prophecy in Israel had its Amoses and its Hoseas, but criticism has long since learned how impossible it is to make hard-and-fast distinctions between prophets of doom and prophets of salvation, and we must beware of dismissing the problem of Jesus and John with a ready-made solution suggested by such or similar distinctions. Men are moulded as much by their experiences as by their environment and their predisposition, and what we need to explain how Jesus could think so highly of John, and at the same time differ so radically from him is some knowledge of experiences stemming from the areas of Jesus' association with the Baptist that might have encouraged his character and background to assert themselves in such a way as to lead his life and thought into new ways without disturbing his loyalty to John. One or two such experiences seem to be recorded in the Synoptic Gospels.

It is a well-known fact that, like many of his serious-minded contemporaries, Jesus interpreted his own age as one of tensions, of stresses and of the workings of great powers. Many of these powers were, as Jesus understood it, Satanic. He may have associated them with the reign of the Herodian dynasts and with the cruel fate of John the Baptist, but above all he saw them at work in the misfortunes and the sufferings of the neglected "poor." Among the noteworthy experiences of his life, as Gospel record gives us ample reason to remember, was this, that such powers gave way before him as a preacher of the coming Kingdom. In these healings and exorcisms, the historicity of which there is not the slightest reason to doubt, we have a range of experience associated with the burden of eschatological expectation that Jesus derived from John, but a range of experience that was apparently not shared by John. What Jesus made of this increment of experience we all know. His reaction is recorded in the familiar saying, "If I by the finger of God cast out demons, then is the Kingdom of God come upon you" (Lk 11:20). This is, of course, not just a casual statement. It is one of those intuitive pronouncements of which mention has previously been made. As such, its function is to suggest new and significant insights into the meaning of the subject with which it deals. What it tells us in this instance is that, confronted with such experiences, Jesus came to realize that the Kingdom whose imminence John proclaimed was actually in a real sense already present.

In such experiences of the presence of the Kingdom, rather than in a break with John on a matter of principle, I suggest we must seek the roots of the most distinctive features of the Christian Gospel, and the basis for the difference between John's and Jesus' preaching. Seen from Jesus' perspective, events since John's day had already advanced rapidly toward the fulfillment of the purpose of history. God's saving will was already in action. *It* was the paramount reality. If that was so, then the time for fasting and withdrawal was gone, and with it the occasion for the re-creation of an exemplary Abrahamic piety. Instead, men must seek to live now, as they would in the future, in spontaneous response to the manifest goodness of their heavenly Father, seeking only his forgiveness while there was still time and the completion of their deliverance from the power of evil. For Jesus himself it followed that, forsaking everything else he must spread the word of God's active intervention in history, pronouncing blessings over those who though "poor," sad, hungry and persecuted would soon find their lot reversed, and pronouncing woes over those whose impenitence made them the inevitable objects of God's righteous anger.

If truly Jesus' own experience of the presence of the Kingdom is the root of the differences between him and John, Jesus' continuing loyalty to the Baptist and the nature of his testimony to John can readily be accounted for. After all, these experiences were associated with the burden of John's proclamation, that the end of the age was at hand. If time had moved on toward the proclaimed fulfillment, that might call for a revision of attitudes, but it did not make John less of a prophet. Yet it is strange that the materials upon which we have to depend for this interpretation of Jesus' departure from John's outlook come out so casually in the record, a bit here and a bit there. We would expect some one narrative, at least, to give us knowledge of a crucial episode in Jesus' life that determined the parting of the ways in thought and practice. Instead, right where we would expect to find it, just before Jesus appears preaching the Gospel, we have the account of his installation in high messianic office. At this point some reflection on the way in which the passage of time and changing interests alter pragmatically the significance of important episodes and materials may be in order. The exorcisms and healings are themselves cases in point. That they were of great significance to both Jesus and the early Church is perfectly clear. For the Church they were primarily proofs of Jesus' divine authorization, as Peter declares when he speaks of Jesus as a man "approved of God among you by miracles and wonders and signs" (Acts 2:22). What they meant for Jesus we would not know save for the good fortune of having the word already used above that interprets them as signs of the powers of God reaching into the world and proving the presence of the Kingdom.

If we were to suppose that an analogous change is reflected in the report of Jesus' baptismal experience, it might be possible to find in this narrative what we need as the occasion of Jesus' departure from John's proclamation. Everything depends here upon the meaning of the statements in which the content of the experience is expressed, and surely these statements could originally have had a broadly eschatological rather than an individual, messianic import. Conceivably what happened was that Jesus, having submitted to baptism in the expectation of the imminence of God's final judgment, did upon his emergence from the water actually see himself standing in the age of fulfillment, the heavens open in token of the presence of God with men, the voice of God speaking to him words of recognition and of acceptance into sonship and the Spirit descending upon him in accordance with the prophecies about the new age. Having submitted to the divine judgment in the symbolic act of baptism, he might thus be said to have been uplifted by it also to an experience of divine redemption.

If there be any value in this suggestion it would imply that the moment of Jesus' baptism by John was also the moment of crucial significance for the development of the new features in Jesus' preaching. The suggestion would provide for the beginning of Jesus' own career an experience more closely analogous to that of his prophetic predecessors, while also simplifying for us in no small degree the problem of the development of his messianic consciousness. That the early Church soon dated his messiahship back to this event, giving the statements that describe the experience a more restricted import, is a natural result of a change in its perspective and of its interest in this facet of Jesus' life and thought.

Yet in interpreting the episode in this way, the Church continued to recognize that Jesus' baptism by John was an all-important moment in its Master's life. We, looking behind that interpretation, might venture to say that John was in effect the reagent by which on the experiential side the elements of Jesus' distinctive Gospel were brought to precipitation.

To what has been inferred from the materials for our

understanding of the relation betwen John and Jesus one additional saying may have something to add. It is the enigmatic word about the violence that the Kingdom of God suffers (Mt 11:12–13 = Lk 16:16).

The word in question is undoubtedly among the most difficult in the Gospels and no attempt will be made here to resolve all its problems, if that be at all possible. But three salient facts about the saying should be clear. The first is that the word interprets history as revealing movement toward the fulfillment of a divinely ordained purpose and divides this movement into periods. The second is that if Matthew has preserved its original import correctly, the word distinguishes three periods in that movement; the first a period of anticipation represented by the prophecies of the Law and the Prophets; the second a period of violence that begins with John, continues to the moment at which Jesus speaks and is not yet at an end; and the third a period unmentioned but implied, when the violence of the present will give way to the peace of fulfillment. The third salient fact about the saying is that, if Matthew has preserved the original sense correctly, the violence is that of hostile Satanic forces assailing the Kingdom from without.[16]

From these facts a number of inferences can legitimately be drawn. The first is that here again the Kingdom is regarded as present. Otherwise it could not be thought of as suffering violence. The second is that John the Baptist stands at the dividing line between the period of anticipation and the period in which the Kingdom is present but in conflict, quite as we might imagine from what has previously been said. The third is that the Kingdom, while present, is for Jesus not a utopia but the manifestation of a divine power opposed by Satanic powers that seek to destroy it. The fourth and last is that while the resolution of the conflict according to God's own will is inevitable and while the operation of God's own powers in the present bids his children rejoice even now in the fulfillment that is to be, men may find their lives maimed and crushed in the turmoil of the titanic struggle characterizing the transition, for violence is the order of the days.

We venture to suggest that this dark and enigmatic saying is born of Jesus' preoccupation with the fate of John and thus belongs to what we know from the Gospels about the relation of the two men. Of John's death Jesus seems to have said, according to Mark (9:13), "they have done to him whatsoever they would," implying that though authorized to be God's spokesman he was nonetheless a victim of the workings of hostile forces. If in his effort to understand John's fate, Jesus came to an understanding of his age in which faith could be reconciled with and triumph over personal tragedy, as our saying suggests, it may be that John the Baptist served him not only as the reagent by which the elements of his distinctive Gospel were brought to precipitation but also as the inspiration for that line of thought that leads from the contemplation of his personal jeopardy toward the conception of his own place in God's plan.

VI

The Later History of the Baptist Movement

DURING his lifetime, we are reliably informed, John the Baptist created a great stir in certain sections of Palestine. "All the country of Judæa and all the people of Jerusalem went out to him," says Mark in his exaggerating but dramatic way (1:5). "Everybody turned to John for they were profoundly stirred by what he said" and "seemed likely to do everything he might counsel," echoes Josephus. The Jewish historian in speaking of John's hold upon the people had in mind particularly his ability to crystallize anti-Herodian sentiment, which made Antipas fear an armed insurrection. Much of the influence that the Baptist wielded in political affairs his death unquestionably brought to an end, but the same was not true in the sphere of religious life. In this sphere his influence continued to exert itself first inside the confines of his native land and later in the world at large, so much so that even in the present its

158

force cannot be said to have spent itself entirely. Without some consideration of this influence it would be impossible either to take the full measure of the man or to interpret correctly the evidence for his life and work.

In the period immediately after John's imprisonment, Jesus seems to have contributed more than any other known individual to the perpetuation of the Baptist's influence. The very fact that, having himself been baptized by John, he made John's imprisonment the occasion for the beginning of a preachment in Galilee (Mk 1:14), the crown land of Herod Antipas, is typical of his attitude and of a movement that refuses to die even when its head has been removed. That Jesus himself took up the theme of the coming eschatological consummation must have helped to allay any doubts that John's imprisonment might have cast on the validity of the wilderness proclamation. Whatever other historical value the story about the delegation sent to Jesus by John from prison may have (Mt 11:2–6; Lk 7:19–23), it presupposes the existence of an attitude of wonder in Baptist circles about John's new-found successor. This can only have been heightened by the encomia of Jesus on John that have already been analyzed, namely, his interpretation of John as Elijah and his references to him as a prophet and more than a prophet, the greatest among those born to this high calling. Jesus defended John's baptism as divinely authorized even in Jerusalem (Mk 11:30), and when the developing contrasts between his own ministry and that of John were made the occasion of adverse com-

ment by those interested in alienating the two movements from each other, Jesus brought the comment out
into the open and remarked on the impossibility of satis-
fying congenital scoffers (Mt 11:18–19; Lk 7:33–35).

The eventual execution of John constituted perhaps
the most serious of all threats to the perpetuation of the
Baptist movement, for it raised inevitably the question
of how, if John had truly been God's authorized agent,
God, being righteous, could have permitted his emissary
to be put to naught. It was the same question that the
disciples of Jesus later had to face, the question that they
answered with the affirmation about the substitutionary
value of the unmerited sufferings of the righteous and
ultimately with the grandiose conception of the vicarious
atonement. John's detractors used the occasion of his
death to develop the suggestion that his disembodied
spirit was serving Jesus as the instrument for the performance of works of black magic, itself no small conces-
sion to John's power.[1] Jesus grappled with the issue in
its more serious form and seems to have reached a solution that ultimately may not have been unimportant,
also, for his thinking about his own fate. The solution
seems to be indicated, as we have seen, in the word about
the violence suffered by the Kingdom of God since the
days of John (Mt 11:12), and would imply that the
death of a man like John is intelligible as a result of the
clash of titanic forces in the period immediately preceding the eschatological consummation.[2] Far from denying
the validity of John's message and his authorization,

John's death as Jesus sees it throws into bold relief the characteristics of the age properly understood. What comfort and strength this explanation may have given to Baptist circles we can only imagine.

Yet it was not only Jesus who was responsible for John's continued influence in the religious life of his people. In no small measure it was the sympathizers of John himself, the large constituency of those baptized by his baptism who carried on where John had been forced to leave off. This we see in part from the statement of Josephus that when, in 36 A.D., Antipas suffered an ignominious defeat at the hands of the Nabatæans in reprisal for his plan to divorce King Aretas' daughter and marry Herodias, the people regarded this defeat as a divine punishment upon the tetrarch for his execution of John.[3] More particularly we see it in certain features of Gospel tradition and in significant aspects of the development of the Christian Church. With these we must concern ourselves in some detail.

Basic to the whole subsequent development of the Baptist movement and its impact upon the Church and Gospel tradition is the fact that John during his lifetime had disciples, a fact duly attested by all strata of Gospel record. Historically the adherence of groups of "followers" to specific individuals is nothing new in the religious life of the Hebrew people. Isaiah 8:16 suggests that the prophets of the Old Testament themselves had "disciples" to whom they might entrust their testimony. What is implied originally in such discipleship is mainly that the person "followed" is recognized as a man of authority, speaking the words of Yahweh. In the later period, beginning apparently in the first century B.C., the discipleship phenomenon begins to play an increasingly large part in Jewish religious life. The great rabbis of the time had disciples; so did Jesus and John, and in the Gospels we even hear of disciples of the Pharisees (Mk 2:18) with whatever justification. Here, it would seem, the discipleship concept has been modified somewhat, perhaps as the result of influences that have their roots ultimately in the impact of Greek educational procedure upon the Orient. The authority of the teacher still depends upon his direct or indirect relation to the revealed will of God, but the term disciple can now also designate one who is in constant attendance upon his teacher as a literal "follower," and whose purpose it is to be "like his master" (Mt 10:24) and to uphold his teacher's authority.[4]

Corresponding, it may be, to these two phases in the development of the discipleship concept is a phenomenon reflected in Gospel record, namely, a distinction that seems to be drawn between disciples in the wider sense of the term as persons who accept Jesus' authority, and disciples in the narrower sense of the term as a group of chosen intimates who accompany Jesus where he goes and are in a special sense the subjects of his instruction. Unless the Christian point of view has clouded the historical picture at this point, we may need to postulate the same phenomenon also for the Baptist movement. The wider circle of John's disciples would be those who in Galilee practiced John's fasting and became the occasion for the question addressed to Jesus on this subject (Mk 2:18), and would normally include Jesus himself and such of his disciples as may have been recruited from among those baptized by John. The narrower circle would embrace those who had been in direct attendance upon John and thus could be supposed to have been sent by the imprisoned John asking Jesus "Art thou he that cometh?" (Mt 11:2–3), who could have buried John's body (Mk 6:29) and could have brought to Jesus news of the Baptist's death (Mt 14:12).

Precisely in what form the Baptist disciples perpetuated John's movement we can only surmise. Separate communal existence of the Essene type it would be rash to attribute at the outset to the Baptist circles, particularly because John himself had apparently no thought of creating inside the Jewish nation a separate nucleus of the true sons of Abraham. What characterized his wider following, at the outset, at least, can only have been the acceptance of his prophecy and his baptism, and the conscious effort to live as a part of a "prepared people." To be a disciple of the Baptist was, therefore, in a sense to be of those who, like Joseph of Arimathæa, were "looking for the Kingdom of God" (Mk 15:43) and who lived accordingly. What it meant to live accordingly we can also know only in part. Fasting and the use of set prayers are the only details of Baptist religious observance of which we have information. As to type, neither of these modes of observance was unique, for fasting was a regular practice among the Pharisees (Lk 18:12), and regulations concerning the daily use of stated prayers were in process of development in Judaism as a whole at this very time. Naturally there may have been in Baptist observance distinctive features that gave it particular significance, but if so, we have no knowledge of them. All we can say on this point is that in all likelihood their prayers were, like the Lord's Prayer, strongly eschatological. Under the circumstances, it is probable that Baptist observance served less to distinguish John's followers from other groups than to provide an element of cohesion between those who acknowledged him as their teacher.

For our knowledge of the further development of the Baptist movement one feature in the evolution of the Christian community is of particular value. This is a transformation that took place in the inner group of Jesus' own disciples. During Jesus' lifetime, it will be recalled, they supported their Master's cause by preaching, and we are told that they even performed exorcisms and healings after his example and in his name (Mk 6:7–13). The personal commitment to Jesus involved in this supporting activity was called into question by his death which, as in the case of the Baptist, could be and by some was understood to imply that he had not truly been authorized by God. Once the disciples through the impact of what we call the "resurrection experiences" had found release from the difficulty, their commitment and the circumstances in which they found themselves required of them a new form of activity, namely, that of "witness," and his "witnesses" they became, to the ends of the earth (Acts 1:8). The close analogy between the two groups suggests that quite the same thing must have happened to the inner company of John's disciples. During his lifetime they could be thought of as engaging in controversy with others of their own people "about purification" (Jn 3:25), which means, of course, upholding the Baptist's requirement of baptism for salvation. After they had resolved the problem posed by his death they must also have become "witnesses."

We have no testimonies of these Baptist "witnesses" and no "Book of Acts" to describe their activities, but from the subsequent developments in the ritual and the tradition of the Christian group we can properly draw two inferences about them. The first is that they perpetuated the use of the rite of baptism as John had practiced it, probably requiring it of all who would associate themselves with their circles and incidentally thereby transforming the rite into one of initiation. This is the necessary presupposition for the introduction of baptism into the Christian community as we shall see later. The second is that they developed, after a period of time no doubt, a sacred legend about John himself. Of this legend, itself a product of the compulsion to witness, we have at least one large piece, the Baptist Infancy Narrative now imbedded in the Lukan Nativity Story.

Having the Infancy Narrative, already dealt with above, we can obtain not a little insight into the piety of the Baptist disciples who created it, their high regard for personal integrity and righteousness and their conviction that these will ultimately be rewarded by God, their deep devotion to the traditional ideals of the priesthood, their belief that through the agency of that priesthood God plans to prepare the fulfillment of his promises, and finally their own allegiance to John as the wonderchild through whom the fulfillment actually is mediated.[5] All these speak eloquently of the piety of the Baptist communities of Judæa, but between them they do not yet exhaust the evidence that the Infancy Narrative is able to provide.

Imbedded in the composite Christian Nativity Story as Luke records it are a number of lyrics long familiar to most as elements of Christian liturgical usage, namely, the canticles commonly called the *Magnificat,* the *Benedictus* and the *Nunc Dimittis.* Of these canticles, at least the *Benedictus,* spoken by Zacharias after the child's birth, is a part of the Baptist Infancy Narrative, but that it was composed particularly for the Infancy Narrative is less likely than that it represents a psalm or a hymn familiar in Baptist usage and here put into the mouth of John's father.[6] Rendered in poetic form the hymn divides itself naturally into two parts, as follows:

> Blessed be the Lord, the God of Israel,
> For he hath visited and wrought redemption for his
>   People.
> And hath raised up a horn of salvation for us

> In the house of David his servant,
> As he spake from of old
> By the mouth of his holy prophets;
> Salvation from our enemies
> And from the hands of all that hate us,
> To show mercy toward our fathers
> And to remember his holy covenant:
> The oath which he sware
> Unto Abraham our father,
> To grant us release from fear,
> Delivered out of the hand of our enemies,
> That we should serve him in holiness
> And in righteousness before him all our days.

> And thou, child, shalt be called
> The prophet of the Most High,
> For thou shalt go before the face of the Lord
> To make ready his ways,
> To give knowledge of salvation unto his people
> In the remission of their sins
> By the tender mercy of our God,
> With which the dayspring from on high shall visit us,
> To shine upon those that sit in darkness and the
>   shadow of death,
> To guide our feet in the way of peace.
>   (Lk 1:68–75, 76–79)

In the first part of the hymn the poet, placing himself in the position of one who sees the divine purposes already accomplished, praises God for the fulfillment of the prophetic hopes and of the promise made to Abraham. The fulfillment turns about the coming of a deliverer from the house of David who leads Israel to triumph over its national enemies, and by so doing releases his people from fear and ushers in an era of righteousness. Thought and terminology are traditional throughout and stand in glaring contrast to the body of the Infancy Narrative where, it will be recalled, the child born of the house of Aaron brings about the inner transformation of his people and thus places God in the position of being able to fulfill his promises (*cf.* Lk 1:14–17). In the second part of the hymn, however, the dominant ideas of the Infancy Narrative come to clear expression, for what the new-born child is to accomplish is release from terror for those oppressed by the darkness of sin and the shadow of death. The release is effected by the revelation of God's merciful compassion which like a great light from on high guides men's footsteps along the road to peace and reconciliation with God. The one who accomplishes this is he in whom are fulfilled the prophecies of Malachi 3:1 about the "messenger" and of Isaiah 40:3 about the "voice in the wilderness."

The contrast between the first and the second part of the *Benedictus* has led to the suggestion that is in effect a traditional Jewish hymn of the Psalms of Solomon type adapted to Baptist use by an addition at the end. This is entirely possible and would explain very well the evidence as it presents itself to us. Two inferences are

in order if the suggestion is deemed acceptable. The first
is that in the circles of the Baptist disciples, as in those
from which the Psalms of Solomon come, the private use
of the Psalter was supplemented by psalms and hymns
of more recent origin adapted to the religious conviction
of the groups. The same phenomenon developed later in
Christian circles. The second inference is that the Baptist
groups that used such hymns have achieved a sense of
positive assurance and of quiet confidence that seems to
push into the background the drastic, threatening aspects
of John's eschatological proclamation. This would be
particularly intelligible if, in their minds, baptism had
meanwhile become as a rite of initiation the instrument
for the "knowledge of salvation" and the "remission of
sins," and if, as the community of those at "peace" with
God, they felt themselves to be in some sense the "prepared people" of the Lord.

It has been suggested by no less a person than Adolf
Harnack that to the repertory of Baptist hymnody used
by the writer of the Christian Nativity Story there should
be added as a second element the *Magnificat* (Lk 1:46–
55):[7]

> My soul doth magnify the Lord
> And my spirit rejoiceth in God my Saviour,
> For he hath looked upon the low estate of his hand-
>   maiden.
>
> For behold from henceforth shall call me blessed
>   All generations,

For he that is mighty hath done to me great things
    And Holy is his name,
And his mercy is unto generations and generations
    On them that fear him.

He hath showed strength with his arm,
He hath scattered the proud in the imagination of
    their heart,
He hath put down the princes from their thrones
    And hath exalted them of low degree.

The hungry he hath filled with good things,
And the rich he hath sent away empty.

He hath given help to Israel his servant,
    That he might remember mercy,
As he spake unto our fathers,
Toward Abraham and his seed forever.

In our Bibles, of course, the *Magnificat* is assigned to
Mary, being spoken by her at the occasion of her visit
to Elisabeth. But there is an old textual variant that
introduces the hymn with the words, "And Elisabeth
said," which would not only be appropriate to the situation but in accord with the sentiments of the lyric. Actually the "low estate of his handmaiden" is a quotation
from I Samuel 1:11 describing there the childless Hannah
from whom it could with great propriety be transferred
to the childless Elisabeth. In the same way, the proudly

presumptuous and the arrogantly wealthy whom God
sets at naught could well be the priestly aristocracy of
Jerusalem, in which case the poor that constitute the true
Israel in its capacity as the "servant" of God would be
the Baptist community in which the ideal of the rural
priesthood as the chosen instrument for the fulfillment
of God's purposes seems to live on, as we have already
seen. All this would, if true, add to our knowledge not
only of Baptist hymnody but also to our understanding
of the growing self-consciousness of the group.

For the further history of the Baptist movement,
certain contemporaneous developments in the history of
the Christian movement are again of basic importance.
These are the removal of the inner circle of Jesus' disciples from Galilee to Jerusalem, their proclamation that
their Master would soon reappear upon the clouds as the
Son of Man, and their ecstatic Pentecostal experiences.
These developments established the Christian Church
in the area where hitherto the Baptist movement had
been the stronger, produced a formulation of the Gospel
about Jesus as the transcendent Messiah that must have
been particularly intelligible to the Baptist communities
by virtue of John's own proclamation, and ushered in a
period in which the followers of Jesus felt themselves
living in the very age of fulfillment prophesied by Joel,
a fact of no small importance to such other groups as
were "looking for the Kingdom of God." The effect of
these developments was to inaugurate a period of close
fraternization between Christian and Baptist groups, a

fraternization which Jesus' own attitude toward the Baptist had done much to prepare.

The fraternization of Christian and Baptist disciples in Judæa in the early years of the Church provides a welcome solution for a series of problems in our knowledge of the life of the early Church and finds therein its validation.

A group of three passages in the early chapters of Acts suggests that the number of Christian believers grew rapidly during the early years of the Church, from 120 (Acts 1:15) to about 3,000 (Acts 2:41) and then to about 5,000 males, which would correspond to about 20,000 persons (Acts 4:4). The numbers are undoubtedly estimated and involve an element of exaggeration. Yet Paul, looking back upon his first visit to Jerusalem as a Christian could speak of the existence even at that time of "the churches (plural) of Judæa" (Gal 1:22). It has always been something of a mystery whence this strength was recruited. The conversion of certain Jews who had at one time lived in the Dispersion and were now temporarily or permanently resident at Jerusalem (Acts 2:5–13; 6:1) is not enough, and what we are told about a "great company" of priests who became "obedient to the faith" (Acts 6:7) remains an enigma. By far the simplest solution is that large numbers of Baptist disciples entered into or were counted as members of Christian fellowship, and if, as the Infancy Narrative suggests, the Baptist cause was well represented among the rural priests, a subsequent enumeration of a "great company" of priests among the Christian believers would be entirely logical.

Important as the association of Christian and Baptist disciples in Judæa may have been for the growing numbers of those who could be counted "believers," it seems to have been still more important for Christian thought and practice. It is clear, for instance, that during his lifetime Jesus rejected as inappropriate the Baptist and the Pharisaic practice of fasting. Yet it is also clear that fasting soon became a regular feature of Christian observance. Its existence in Christian circles is documented not only in the Didache (8:1) but also at a much earlier time in the Palestinian Church by the familiar passage Mark 2:20. In the context, it will be recalled, Jesus has just affirmed that just as little as a bridegroom's attendants can fast at the occasion of a wedding, so little can he and his disciples fast, living as they are in the glorious days when the promises of the coming of the Kingdom are being fulfilled. To this, the Christian preacher who transmitted the paradigmatic narrative has added an observation in which Jesus has himself become the bridegroom and in which it is said, "When the bridegroom shall be taken away from them . . . then will they fast in that day." The passage can be quoted to show that Christian fasting began after Easter and also in all probability that originally it was celebrated on Friday, the day on which the "bridegroom" was actually "taken away." Since fasting was, as we have already seen, a regular feature of Baptist observance, it is entirely possible that, whatever the explanation of the particular day chosen, the practice itself entered the life of the Church as the result of the entrance of extensive Baptist elements into the Christian fellowship.

More important as a feature of later Christian practice is, of course, the use of the rite of baptism. If we have interpreted the evidence on this point correctly, it would seem that Jesus himself did not baptize. Indeed, with the type of itinerant ministry which he conducted baptism would have been virtually impossible either for him or for his disciples, since sufficient water was not everywhere to be found in Palestine. Yet it is evident that baptism became a regular element of Christian usage sufficiently early to be of equal significance in Gentile and Jewish Christian circles, to suggest that Jesus himself commanded it in the course of the "resurrection appearances" (Mt 28:19), and to create the vague impression that Jesus himself had at one time practiced it (Jn 3:26). Precisely how this change came about we can only conjecture, but the most plausible suggestion is that it, too, resulted from the participation of disciples of John in the life of the early Church. If the largest increase in the number of the "believers" during the first days of the Church came from the Baptist circles of Judæa, and if, as we have suggested, baptism had been perpetuated in these circles as a requirement for admission to them, the mere fact that most of the members of the expanded Christian fellowship had themselves been baptized may have given rise to the conviction that all who aspired to admission to it must be baptized also. This would account for the initiatory character which the rite had in early Christian usage. Of course, baptism as practiced in the new fellowship also took on certain new features, and among these the use of the name of Jesus was apparently the earliest (Acts 8:16).

Association with erstwhile Baptist disciples in one fellowship had still other effects upon those who were Jesus' followers. From their Baptist brethren they received John's Infancy Narrative, which eventually found its parallel in the story of Jesus' birth, some elements of Baptist hymnody and above all a goodly number of the words of John. The words of John apparently came to the knowledge of the Christian group at a very early date, for some of the more striking of them, like the word about the "generation of vipers" and the word about the "two baptisms" were so deeply imbedded in the tradition that they came to be regarded as words of Jesus himself, as we have already had occasion to see.

Eventually, our sources teach us, the period of fraternization ended, giving way to one of intense rivalry between the Christian Church and certain Baptist nuclei. The protagonists on the Baptist side can have been only a fraction of John's erstwhile following, representing only those elements of the community that had not meanwhile been absorbed in the Church, but the struggle was the more bitter just on that account.

Precisely what the circumstances were that occasioned the change is not entirely clear, but two developments in Christian thought and practice certainly played a part. The first was the belief that the Church's rite of baptism conferred the Holy Spirit, the power of the new age and its regenerate life, and the second, the conviction that the Church was the True Israel, the Ecclesia, the company of the redeemed. Both conceptions were, of course, foreign to the Baptist point of view. We do not know exactly when these ideas crystallized in the Church, but their effects are already so clearly visible in events recorded in the Book of Acts that we should probably assign to the forties of the first century of our era.[8] If so, the period of fraternization cannot have lasted much more than a decade.

What we know about the Baptist-Christian conflict of the last half of the Apostolic Age is to be inferred from the way in which the materials of Gospel tradition have been pointed by those who used and defended them in this period of controversy and through whom they came to the Evangelists. Judging by this pointing it would appear that those Baptist faithful who could not go along with the more recent developments in the conviction and the practice of the Church attacked the foundations of its self-assurance from at least two angles. The first was the matter of precedence, where the Baptist claim was that John had been the first to appear upon the scene, preceding Jesus in time and therefore deserving primary allegiance on the part of the faithful in Israel. The second was that Jesus had himself been baptized by John, which implied naturally that Jesus was, in fact, John's disciple and that John's baptism had been normative for Jesus himself.

The Christians on their part were sharp in their denial of the validity of these arguments. Having meanwhile learned to interpret John as the Forerunner not of the transcendent Messiah but of the historical Jesus, they developed within the framework of the Nativity Story the episode that told how the babe in Elisabeth's womb leaped in salutation at the occasion of Mary's visit and how Elisabeth confessed her inability to understand why she should be honored by a visit from the mother of her Lord (Lk 1:41–43). The point made in this story is that precedence is not to be determined chronologically and that the unborn John himself recognized this fact. Eventually the controversy over the matter of precedence brought about certain changes in the Baptist's saying about the "one who comes after." The first change in the saying, as we have seen, was to give the word a confessional character, making it a witness to the might of the one to come.[9] In this confessional form the saying was applied by the Christians, of course, to the historical Jesus. The final change is recorded in the Fourth Gospel where the word is made to read, "After me there comes one who was before me, for he is first in relation to me" (Jn 1:13, 30). Here Jesus' pre-existence is made the basis of his precedence over John.

As for Jesus' baptism by John this was interpreted by the Christians as demonstrating not John's superiority or the sufficiency of the Baptist rite but rather Jesus' own willingness to show the exemplary piety that John had demanded. The position taken was brought to expression in story form, as so often in the type of circles with which we are dealing, giving rise to the additional episode in Matthew's account of Jesus' baptism (Mt 3:14–15). Here, it will be recalled, John tries to prevent Jesus from undergoing his baptism saying that he needs rather to be baptized by Jesus and expressing wonder that Jesus should come to him in words that echo his mother's sentiments. Jesus' reply, indicating that he feels obligated to be exemplary in the fulfillment of all righteousness, implies that he thinks of John's baptism as a "good work," but nothing more. Eventually, so the Fourth Gospel tells us, the baptism of Jesus by John came to be regarded by the Christians as a special favor done for John, so that John might recognize in Jesus the one who took precedence over him and might thus point him out to others (Jn 1:29–34).

While thus refuting the position taken by the loyalist Baptist groups, those who were engaged in the struggle on the Christian side apparently launched out in counter attacks against what they may well have regarded as Baptist presumptuousness. One of the positions they seem to have taken in this connection is that Jesus' superiority over John is reflected in the Mighty Works which he performed. The argument is germane to the life of the early Church for it was preaching Jesus as a "man affirmed by signs and wonders" (Acts 2:22), and probably consisted of nothing more than the affirmation that while

Jesus did Mighty Works, John did not, hence was not Jesus' superior. Out of this argument, it may well be, there came ultimately the story about the delegation that John sent to Jesus from prison (Mt 11:2–6; Lk 7:19–23). In the story, it will be recalled, John hears about Jesus' Mighty Works and at once asks himself whether this does not mean that Jesus is the one whose coming is proclaimed. He thereby adopts the Christian position. Jesus' reply to the disciples of John who raise this question with him has always been something of an enigma, seen as an element of Christian witness, for in merely pointing back to the Mighty Works themselves, it fails to advance the narrative beyond the point where it began. Seen as a piece of an anti-Baptist polemic that turned on the very question of Mighty Works, this feature of the story is entirely intelligible, for it underlines the importance of the deeds in question. In the Fourth Gospel, finally, the argument reaches its ultimate formulation in that the crowds in the very region where John first baptized are said to flock to Jesus declaring that John had performed no miracles but that his witness to Jesus was in every respect true (Jn 10:40–41).

One further aspect of the Christian effort to cope with the non-cooperating Baptist groups may be noted. Apparently, by making John the Forerunner not of the transcendent Messiah but of the historical Jesus, they eventually were led to ask themselves where this left John in his relation to the Kingdom of God. The question is appropriate to circles which regarded themselves in a very real sense as the community of the redeemed already living in the age of fulfillment. The initial response to the question seems to have been to assign John to a place outside the pale, to make of him a Moses who had glimpsed but not entered the Promised Land. This position seems to be reflected in the Lukan version of the word of Jesus about the Kingdom of God suffering violence, a version in which, it will be recalled, John is associated with the period of the Law and the Prophets and where the preaching of the Kingdom begins only after that period has come to an end (Lk 16:16).[10] It is clearly set forth in the supplement which says that in spite of this fact the little in the Kingdom are greater than John (Mt 11:11; Lk 7:28).[11] Interesting as this exclusion of John from the pale of the Kingdom and the Church is, it was not the only inference drawn from John's assignment to the Forerunner role. The Fourth Evangelist, as is commonly known, reversed the procedure, welcomed John back into the fold and elevated him in this connection to the position of the first Christian confessor and witness (Jn 1:19–36; *cf.* also Jn 5:32–36). It is interesting in this connection to see how in his capacity as first witness John himself admits that he must become of lesser and lesser importance (Jn 3:30) and how he gives up voluntarily any claim to being Elijah or a prophet (Jn 1:21). Here the wheel has completed a full turn and John, by being absorbed into the company of confessors, has lost all the individuality he had at the outset. Only a still small Voice in the Wilderness remains.

It would be of great interest and value to gain from contemporary Baptist sources material for the corroboration or correction of the historical developments reconstructed from Gospel record, and to view the changing Baptist-Christian relations from the Baptist point of view. Unfortunately, this privilege is denied us. If our analysis of the Christian tradition is correct, we must infer that of the Baptist circles in Palestine, some resisted absorption in the Christian movement successfully, and eventually rejected association with the Christian faith because it tended to undermine the significance of John and his baptism. To maintain their position the Baptist circles apparently questioned the validity of faith in Jesus as the messianic judge about whose coming John had spoken. The evidence of the New Testament suggests that to maintain their position they also enhanced the significance of John himself as the object of faith. What the positive basis for the elevation of John above the rank of the returned Elijah may have been, we do not know, but the denials of John that he is the Messiah, echoed in Luke and in the Fourth Gospel, are too vehement to permit any doubt that messianic rank was eventually claimed for him by certain of his adherents. The writer of the *Clementine Recognitions* makes the familiar statement that "one of John's disciples declared John to be the Messiah and not Jesus" (I 60).

That in the period to which the *Clementine Recognitions* belong, the Baptist faith had already transplanted itself from Palestine into the wider reaches of the Orient forms a necessary presupposition for the further developments still to be chronicled.[12] These developments, so far as we can trace them in the earlier sources, turn mainly about the use of the rite of baptism in syncretistic sects. We hear about syncretistic sects that adopted the rite first in the *Dialogue* of Justin Martyr and thereafter continuously in the writings of the anti-heretical Fathers, Irenæus, Hegesippus, Hippolytus and Epiphanius. They include Menander and his disciples, the Dositheans, the Simonians, the Marcosians, Justinus and his sect, the Naasenes, Sethians, Elchasaites, Nazareans, Sampseans and Masobotheans.[13] The texts provide evidence for a distribution of the sectarian use of baptism over Asia Minor and Syria, and this distribution we can extend to include Mesopotamia and Egypt with the help of the new Manichean documents and the *Apostolic Constitutions*.

The appearance of the baptismal rite in these syncretistic circles is undoubtedly in no small measure the result of its prominence in Christian usage. On the other hand, Irenæus suggests that the earliest of the sectaries to use it in Syria, namely, Menander, was a disciple of Simon Magus, and according to Acts, Simon himself received only that early form of Christian baptism that was in all important respects the baptism of John and was later so-called by the writer of Acts himself (Acts 8:9–13; 19:3). In the later Simonian *Apophasis Megale*, moreover, John's words about the axe at the root of the tree and about the chaff to be burned by the fire are put to important use in support of the Simonian theology, and in the very late Mandaic texts there is preserved a tradition about John's baptism which in large part is independent of Christian sources.[14] All this suggests that in the syncretistic developments of the second and third centuries the Baptist movement shared with the Church in popularizing the use of the baptismal rite. Indeed, the chances are that such elements of John's following as left Palestine and established themselves in other parts of the Orient became syncretistic themselves in their outlook and were transformed into Baptist sectaries, under whatever name. Apparently baptism changed its meaning entirely in the new environment, a Syrian theogony, in which divine powers are called into being out of the primordial deep, providing the suggestion for its transformation into a rite of deification. If what we have said before about the symbolic and dramatic character of John's baptism is correct, the act could have been made to symbolize deification in a syncretistic environment quite as readily as, in a Christian environment, it was made to symbolize participation in the death and resurrection of Jesus.

It is interesting to note that during the whole of the second and third centuries, while the forces of syncretism were thus apparently capitalizing upon the Baptist rite, Christian legend and the Christian Church Fathers have very little to say about John. It may be that he was being exploited too effectively by the "heretics" to make him an attractive subject of Christian thought and speculation. But when in the fourth century the Gnostic crisis

183

had passed, John suddenly became again for the Church a very important person. Festival days celebrated in his honor find a place in the Church's liturgical calendar. Churches and martyria are erected in commemoration of him particularly at Samaria, Alexandria and Constantinople, but also in other widely separated parts of the Byzantine Orient. Above all, there develops at this time a great body of Baptist legend that soon spreads over the entire eastern Christian world. It has left traces of itself in a vast body of literature that includes the Protevangelium of James, the late Syriac Life of John, the Zacharias apocrypha, poems of the Syrian Church Fathers, Armenian, Coptic and Syriac hagiographs, Arabic Shi'ite legends and the works of Byzantine theologians.[15]

No one has yet threaded his way through the entire maze of this later Baptist legend, but in the main it would seem to concern itself with three themes. The first is that of John's infancy, where the emphasis falls upon his continuous sojourn in the wilderness that Luke himself had already brought into the picture (Lk 1:80). John's early sojourn in the desert is occasioned by the murder of Zacharias under circumstances suggested by the story of the slaughter of the innocents, and becomes the setting for many acts of supernatural intervention. The second theme is John's life as an adult, where the tendency is to transform the Baptist into the ideal prototype of the Christian hermit and ascetic. The third is the ultimate fate of John's body and head, the miraculous discovery, travels and ultimate disposition of which provide a wealth of opportunity for the exercise of pious imagination.

A knowledge of these materials would seem to be of significance only for the student of Byzantine hagiography, yet such is not the case. Actually, what they tell us about the growth of the tradition in the later period provides an important foil for the developments of the earlier period with which we have here largely concerned ourselves. More than that, it gives the necessary perspective upon the two attempts made in recent years to change radically the historical picture of John the Baptist by the use of later sources. Of these attempts, the one is that of Eisler, who introduced the material of the "Slavonic" Josephus, and the other is that of Reitzenstein, who fell back on the literature of the Baptist sect of later Mesopotamia that we know as the Mandeans. If both these attempts to reinterpret John have served to confuse the issue for students of the New Testament, it is because both they and the proponents of the hypotheses failed to follow the course of the ever-changing tradition through the later centuries of its history. Seen in the light of later Baptist legend, the so-called "Slavonic" Josephus reflects beside their historical absurdities only the efforts of the Byzantine writers to visualize John in terms of the hermit ideal.[16] Seen in the light of the later history of the Baptist movement the Mandaic texts combine merely the syncretistic use of baptism developed in the second and third centuries with the material provided largely by Syriac hagiographa and Arabic legend.[17] Neither can be said to yield new information more valuable than that contained in the Gospels.

For the interpretation of John as for that of any other figure of religious significance, it is important to keep in mind not only the essential facts about his life, work and thought so far as we can know them, but also the impact he made upon his contemporaries and upon later generations. The religious relationship, since it has its roots in the interplay between man and something greater than himself, and involves in some measure the self-impartation of the divine to the human, is a dynamic thing, giving impulse and movement to life and unleashing forces that affect the lives of others. For this reason its measure cannot be taken exclusively by a record of the circumstances under which it established itself or by a philosophical interpretation of the meaning of those circumstances. To these we need to add in each instance some consideration of its effects upon the developing pattern of human life. Measured by any such standard, John the Baptist does not belong to the greatest figures of religious history, for the forces he released lost much of their original import within a few generations after his death and have survived since that time only within the framework of impulses emanating from one greater than he. Yet for his own day and generation John undoubtedly had a profound significance, the significance of a heroic figure, stern, forbidding, provocative, fired with the heat of prophetic passion, calling men to self-humiliation before the throne of God. The fact that, in this capacity, he so deeply affected Jesus, his greater successor, assures him a place among the immortals of religious history.

Notes

Abbreviations

AASOR, Annual of the American Schools of Oriental Research.
ATR, Anglican Theological Review.
BASOR, Bulletin of the American Schools of Oriental Research.
HUCA, Hebrew Union College Annual.
JAOS, Journal of the American Oriental Society.
JBL, Journal of Biblical Literature.
QDAP, Quarterly of the Department of Antiquities of Palestine.
REJ, Revue des Études Juives.
ZNTW, Zeitschrift für die neutestamentliche Wissenschaft.

Notes

CHAPTER 1. JOHN THE BAPTIST AND THE WILDERNESS

1. The most recent monographs written in English are still those of
   A. T. Robertson, *John the Loyal* (1911) and A. Blakiston, *John
   the Baptist and his Relation to Jesus* (1912). Meanwhile there
   have appeared in other languages: M. Dibelius, *Die urchristliche
   Überlieferung von Johannes dem Täufer* (1911), M. Goguel, *Au
   seuil de l'Evangile, Jean Baptiste* (1928), E. Lohmeyer, *Das
   Urchristentum, 1. Buch: Johannes der Täufer* (1932) and Père
   D. Buzy, *S. Jean Baptiste* (1922), the last-mentioned available
   also in the English translation of J. M. T. Barton under the title
   Life of St. John the Baptist (1933).
2. For purposes of reference the New Testament materials dealing
   with John the Baptist are here listed in accordance with the
   sources from which they are taken:

   A. Material supplied by Mk, and re-used for the most part by
   his successors, Mt and Lk.

   1. Mk 1:2–8. *John the Forerunner,* his person and preach-
      ing. *Cf.* also Mt 3:1–6, Lk 3:1–6; 15–16.
   2. Mk 1:9–11. *Jesus is baptized by John. Cf.* also Mt
      3:13–17; Lk 3:21–22.
   3. Mk 1:14. *John's imprisonment, a synchronism. Cf.* Mt
      4:12, 17.
   4. Mk 2:18. *John's disciples fast: an observation. Cf.* Mt
      9:14; Lk 5:33.
   5. Mk 6:14–16. *John "raised" from the dead. Cf.* Mt
      14:1–2; Lk 9:7–9.
   6. Mk 6:17–29. *John's preaching against Herod, his execu-
      tion and burial. Cf.* Mt 14:3–12; Lk 3:19–20.
   7. Mk 8:27–28. *Jesus is John the Baptist. Cf.* Mt 16:14;
      Lk 9:19.
   8. Mk 9:11–13. *John the Baptist was Elijah. Cf.* Mt
      17:10–13.
   9. Mk 11:29–33. *John's baptism, was it a human or a
      divine institution? Cf.* Mt 21:25–27; Lk 20:4–7.

   B. Material supplied by a Second Source, common to Mt and
   Lk.

   1. Mt3:7–10 = Lk 3:7–9. *John's preaching of repentance.*
   2. Mt 3:11–12 = Lk 3:15–17. *John's preaching of the
      Messiah.*

3. Mt 11:2–6 = Lk 7:18–23. *John's inquiry from prison.*
4. Mt 11:7–11 = Lk 7:24–28. *Jesus' testimony to John.*
5. Mt 11:16–19 = Lk 7:31–35. *John and Jesus in the eyes of their contemporaries.*
6. Mt 11:12 = Lk 16:16. *John and the Kingdom in an era of violence.*

C. Materials proper to Matthew
1. Mt 3:14–15. *The discussion at the baptism of Jesus.*
2. Mt 11:14–15. *John is Elijah.*
3. Mt 21:32. *John's following. Cf. Lk 7:29–30.*

D. Materials proper to Luke
1. Lk 1:5–25, 57–66, 67–80. *The birth of John.*
2. Lk 3:1–2. *The date of John's preaching.*
3. Lk 3:10–14. *John's ethical teaching.*
4. Lk 3:19–20. *John's imprisonment: a statement of fact.*
5. Lk 7:29–30. *John's converts. Cf. Mt 21:32.*
6. Lk 11:1. *John teaches prayer: an observation.*

E. The Acts of the Apostles
1. Acts 1:5 and 11:16. *John baptized with water: a saying.*
2. Acts 1:22 and 10:37. *John's baptism: a reference.*
3. Acts 13:24–25. *John and the coming of Jesus.*
4. Acts 19:1–7. *John's baptism at Ephesus.*

F. The Fourth Gospel
1. Jn 1:6–8. *John the witness to the Light.*
2. Jn 1:15. *The nature of John's witness.*
3. Jn 1:19–40. *An account of John's witness.*
4. Jn 3:22–30. *The implications of John's witness.*
5. Jn 5:33–36. *Jesus, the Jews and John's witness.*
6. Jn 10:40–41. *Those across the Jordan and John's witness.*

3. For convenience' sake the single passage from Josephus (*Antiquities* XVIII, 5, 2 = §§ 116–119 ed. Naber) is quoted here in full:

. . . but some of the Jews believed that Herod's army was destroyed by God, God punishing him very justly for John called the Baptist, whom Herod had put to death. For John was a pious man, and he was bidding the Jews who practiced virtue and exercised righteousness toward each other and piety toward God, to come together for baptism. For thus, it seemed to him, would baptismal ablution be acceptable, if it were

used not to beg off from sins committed, but for the purification of the body when the soul had previously been cleansed
by righteous conduct. And when everybody turned to John—
for they were profoundly stirred by what he said—Herod
feared that John's so extensive influence over the people might
lead to an uprising (for the people seemed likely to do everything he might counsel). He thought it much better, under the
circumstances, to get John out of the way in advance, before
any insurrection might develop, than for himself to get into
trouble and be sorry not to have acted, once an insurrection
had begun. So because of Herod's suspicion, John was sent as
a prisoner to Machærus, the fortress already mentioned, and
there put to death. But the Jews believed that the destruction
which overtook the army came as a punishment for Herod,
God wishing to do him harm (Translation of H. St. John
Thackeray in the Loeb Classical Library edition).

4. For the theory that a biographical account of the Baptist composed by one of his disciples was used by Josephus in his "Capture of Jerusalem" as known from the "Slavonic" version of
Josephus' Jewish War *cf.* R. Eisler, *The Messiah Jesus and John
the Baptist* (1931) pp. 223–226. For the theory that a Baptist
apocalypse antedating the Second Source is preserved in the
first and second tracts of the *Right Ginza,* a sacred book of the
Mandeans, *cf.* R. Reitzenstein, "Das mandäische Buch des Herrn
der Grösse und die Evangelienüberlieferung," *Sitzungsberichte
der Heidelberger Akademie der Wissenschaften,* 1919, Abhand-
lung 12. The following Gospel materials have been said to come
from written Baptist sources: (a) Lk 1:5–25, 57–80. So first D.
Völter, "Die Apokalypse des Zacharias im Evanglius des Lucas,"
Theologische Tijdschrift XXX (1896), pp. 244–269, and more
recently M. Goguel, *Jean Baptiste,* p. 74; (b) Mt 3:11–12 (*cf.*
Lk 3:16–17). So Goguel, *Jean Baptiste,* p. 42, who refers to J.
Wellhausen, *Einleitung in die ersten drei Evangelien,* 2. ed.
(1911), p. 65, probably without actual justification; (c) Jn
1:1–6a, 10b–11, 14, 16a, 17. So H. H. Schaeder, *Studien zum
antiken Synkretismus aus Iran und Griechenland* (1927), pp.
306–341, esp. p. 330.
5. Recent discoveries of manuscript deposits both in Palestine
(Dead Sea Scrolls) and in Egypt (Coptic Gnostic Documents)
show how extensive was the body of written material in the
hands of sectarian groups and suggest extreme caution in denying to the Baptist movement a "literature" of its own. Though
much of this postulated Baptist "literature" would doubtless be-

long to the syncretistic phases of the development of the movement, and thus to the second century, some of it could conceivably
have gone back to Judæa and the period before the destruction
of the Temple. The proper period for the beginnings of such a
"literature" would be the years after the break between the
Christian and the Baptist disciples and most of the material incorporated in the Gospels seems to belong to the preceding
period of fraternization between the two groups. Since this period
was apparently very short, extending, perhaps, only to the reign
of Herod Agrippa, it is likely that the material incorporated in
the Gospel tradition came by word of mouth. For the historical
picture of the development of the two groups see Chapter VI
below.

6. See Mk 1:4 = Mt 3:1 and Lk 3:2; Mt 11:7 = Lk 7:24; Jn 1:23.

7. On later Baptist legend see Chapter VI below. It should be noted
that Luke has changed the picture of Mark and the Second
Source in having John's wilderness sojourn end at 3:2 when he
begins to act as Jesus' Forerunner. The period of segregation is
thus a preparation for high calling as in the case of Apollonius
of Tyana, who spent five years in silence before entering upon his
life's work. *Cf.* Philostratus, *Vita Apollonii* I, 14.

8. On the traditional Hebrew usage *cf.* Père F.-M. Abel, *Géographie
de la Palestine* (1933), p. 436. On Matthew's use of geographical
material *cf.* C. C. McCown, "Gospel Geography, Fact, Fiction
and Truth," *JBL*, LX, 1 (1940), pp. 9–13.

9. On the probable location of Bethany beyond Jordan *cf.* G. Dal-
man, *Sacred Sites and Ways* (1935), pp. 87–93. The variant
"Bethabara," meaning "house of the ford," was preferred by
Origen but was probably interpretative rather than transcrip-
tional, though it may well represent a good acquaintance with
changed circumstances (relocation of the village or change in
terminology if not nomenclature). For the location of Ænon
(*'ainun* meaning "springs") near Salim *cf.* Père F.-M. Abel, *Géographie* pp. 142, 447 and Fig. 7. As the site of the town of Salim
near these springs *Umm el-'Amdan* is to be preferred over *Tell
er-Ridghah*. *Cf.* W. F. Albright, *BASOR* No. 19 (Oct., 1925),
p. 18. The suggestion of Kundsin (*Topologische Überlieferungs-
stoffe im Johannesevangelium* [1925], pp. 20–27, 73–75) that the
place names appear in the Fourth Gospel because groups of
Baptist disciples were still located there in the Evangelist's day
is not without merit. If so it may well be that they endeavored
to perpetuate the founder's rite in the area where he practiced
it before them.

10. John's basic association with the southern part of the Jordan valley is reflected in the statement that "all Judæa and the people of Jerusalem" went out to hear him (Mk 1:5). A. T. Olmstead has suggested that John moved northward, across the river, to Ænon because of his quarrel with Herod Antipas (*Jesus in the Light of History* [1942], p. 94). If so, he ultimately moved back again.

11. It is uncertain whether by "wild honey" Mark means honey collected by wild bees or the gum exuded by certain types of trees. On the distinction and the dietary laws in question *cf.* H. L. Strack-P. Billerbeck, *Kommentar zum Neuen Testament aus Talmud u. Midrasch I* (1922), pp. 98–101. In the Byzantine legends which the "Slavonic" Josephus reflects, the Baptist is said to subsist on cane and roots and fruits. The text is conveniently accessible in the Appendix to Vol. III (1928) of Thackeray's edition of Josephus in the Loeb Classical Library. See in this instance p. 645. The Syriac *Life of John* (ed. A. Mingana, *Woodbroke Studies I* [1927], p. 245) speaks of grass and wild honey. Apparently there was some objection to the idea of John's eating locusts. The legends omit the locusts and thus make John a vegetarian.

12. *Cf.* my article, "Was Jesus accused of Necromancy?" *JBL* LIX, 2 (1940), pp. 147–157.

13. Against Lk 1:15, which might well be true in fact under wilderness conditions but without the implications seen in the statement by Luke's informants and by modern interpreters. *E.g.*, A. T. Robertson, *John the Loyal*, p. 10, and A. Blakiston, *John the Baptist*, p. 252. Luke's informant like the Byzantine legends (see Note 11) is pressing circumstance to create new detail. This is typical of legend.

14. So the Syriac *Life of John* (ed. A. Mingana), p. 239.

15. See particularly M. Dibelius, *Johannes der Taufer*, pp. 67–77; *idem*, "Jungfraunsohn und Krippenkind," *Sitzungsberichte der Heidelberger Akademie der Wissenschaften* 1932, Heft 4; G. Erdmann, *Die Vorgeschichten des Lukas- und Mattäusevangeliums* (1932). The analogous episodes and the materials that are used to combine the two independent narratives can best be shown in tabular form, as follows:

John	Jesus
1:5–25 Annunciation of the birth of John to Zacharias by Gabriel.	1:26–38 Annunciation of the birth of Jesus to Mary by Gabriel.

1:39–56 Visit of Mary to Elisabeth.

1:57–66 Birth, circumcision and naming of John, with attendant wonders.	2:1–21 Birth, circumcision and naming of Jesus, with attendant wonders.
1:67–80 Praise of the infant John by the inspired Zacharias. Growth of the child.	2:22–40 Praise of the infant Jesus by the inspired Simeon and Hannah. Growth of the child.

2:41–52 Proof of the superior importance of the child Jesus from his behavior in the Temple.

16. The *Babylonian Talmud* (Yoma 39b) and the *Palestinian Talmud* (Yoma 5, 42c) tell the story of the mysterious figure in white garments that accompanied Simeon the Righteous of the Great Sanhedrin (c. 300 B.C.) into the Holy of Holies on each Day of Atonement, while Josephus (*Antiquities* XIII, 10, 3 = § 282) relates how the high priest Hyrcan I (135–104 B.C.) heard a voice from heaven while performing the incense sacrifice in the Temple. What happens in these instances is a mark and sign of the importance and the exemplary piety of the persons in question.

17. It will be recalled that the demand for a sign was regarded as improper in Christian circles as well. *Cf.* Mt 12:39.

18. On the distinction see the discussion of M. Dibelius, *From Tradition to Gospel* (1935), pp. 104–109.

19. See particularly in the Testaments of the Twelve Patriarchs, Testament of Levi 18, and in general W. Bousset-H. Gressmann, *Religion des Judentums* 3. ed. (1926), pp. 223, 226.

20. Pesachim 57a. The translation is that of I. Epstein in the Soncino edition (1938), p. 285. On the identity of the priests in question *cf.* E. Schuerer, *Geschichte des jüdischen Volkes*, etc., II (1907), pp. 269–271.

21. The material in Josephus will be found in *Antiquities* XX, 8, 8 = § 181 and 9, 2 = § 207. The reference in the Talmud is again Pesachim 57a. On the subject in general see L. Finkelstein, *The Pharisees* I (1938), pp. 22–23.

22. See also Is 34:14; Tobit 8:3.

23. See especially Josephus, *Antiquities* XX, 5, 1 = §§ 97–98; XX, 8, 6 = §§ 169–72 and XX, 8, 10 = § 188.

24. On the interpretation of the elaborate synchronism of Lk 3:1
cf. my article, "Olmstead's Chronology of the Life of Jesus," *ATR*
XXIV, 4 (1942), pp. 344–346. R. Eisler, *The Messiah Jesus,* pp.
288–311, has questioned the value of the Lukan synchronism but
the new chronological pattern that he has set up on the basis
of the "Slavonic" Josephus has not recommended itself widely.

CHAPTER II. JOHN'S PREACHING: THE PROCLAMATION

1. On the implications of the three words κηρύσσω, κράζω and
   μαρτυρέω see G. Kittel, *Theologisches Wörterbuch zum Neuen
   Testament* (1933 ff.), s. v., and E. Lohmeyer, *Johannes der Täufer,*
   pp. 44–45. For the statement of Josephus cf. above, Chapter I,
   note 3.
2. The notable exception is the Mandean legend which has John
   address long harangues to the Jews, to Jesus and to his own followers. Though they preserve correctly the eschatological frame
   of reference, they are devoid of historical value. See particularly
   Das Johannesbuch der Mandäer, ed. M. Lidzbarski (1915), chaps.
   19–33.
3. On the attitude of the Fourth Evangelist to John, first interpreted correctly by G. Baldensperger, *Der Prolog des vierten
   Evangeliums* (1898), see now M. Dibelius, *Johannes der Täufer,*
   pp. 119–123, M. Goguel, *Jean Baptiste,* pp. 75–95, E. Lohmeyer,
   Johannes der Täufer, pp. 26–30 and especially E. C. Colwell,
   John Defends the Gospel (1936), pp. 32–39. Characteristic is the
   Fourth Evangelist's treatment of the two Baptist sayings on the
   Mightier One and on the two baptisms (see below) which are
   telescoped and so transformed as to make the first yield a witness
   to Jesus' pre-existence. See most recently R. Bultmann, *Das
   Johannesevangelium* (1939), p 51, on Jn 1:15 and 30.
4. In his *Geschichte der synoptischen Tradition* 2. ed. (1933), pp.
   123–155, R. Bultmann suggests that Mt 3:7–10 = Lk 3:7–9 and
   Lk 3:10–14 are words of Jesus transferred to John. This is ar-
   bitrary and rests upon an erroneous conception of the relation of
   the Baptist and the Christian movement in the days of the early
   Church.
5. Hos 13:3; Is 17:13; 29:5; Ps 1:4; 35:5; Job 21:18.
6. For the use of the threshing-floor metaphor in rabbinic times cf.
   the parable of R. Abun (c. 370 A.D.) in which the rival claims of
   the nations are compared to the rivalry between the straw, the
   chaff and the stubble, the lesson being that the coming of the

threshing-floor (God's judgment) will settle the issue. Song of Songs Rabbah 7:3 accessible in the new translation of the Soncino Press, *Midrash Rabbah* IV (1939), p. 284.

7. On sacred trees in Semitic religion generally see Robertson Smith, *Religion of the Semites* 3. ed. (1927), pp. 189–196. The *ashera* is, of course, the classic tree symbol of the Canaanite cultus.

8. Sirach 6:4; 23:25; Wisdom of Solomon 4:3–5.

9. *E.g.* J. Wellhausen, *Evangelium Matthaei* (1904), p. 5, A. Loisy, *Évangiles synoptiques* I (1907), p. 395, and in general K. L. Schmidt, *Rahmen der Geschichte Jesu* (1919), pp. 25–26.

10. See G. Kittel, *Theologisches Wörterbuch* s. v. ἔχιδνα and F. S. Bodenheimer, *Animal Life in Palestine* (Jerusalem, 1935), pp. 184–191. The craftiness which M. J. Lagrange adds to bolster the suggestion of improper motives (*Évangile selon Luc* [1927], p. 106), is characteristic rather of the snake (ὄφις).

11. *Cf.* the use of the word, namely ὑποδείκνυμι, in Lk 6:47; 12:5; Acts 9:16; 20:35.

12. See the passages quoted in Chapter I, note 23, and in general H. St. J. Thackeray, *Josephus, the Man and the Historian* (1929), pp. 87–98 and P. Volz, *Jüdische Eschatologie* (1903), pp. 209–210.

13. In the subordinate clause the substitution of "sandal" (Jn 1:27) for "sandals," of "worthy" (Acts 13:25, Jn 1:27) for "fit," of "carry" (Mt 3:11) for "loosen," the omission of "thong" (Mt 3:11, Acts 13:25) and the addition of "bend down" (Mk 1:17) are all likely to be secondary.

14. On the Fourth Evangelist's handling of the main clause see above, note 3.

15. See E. Lohmeyer, "Zur Evangelischen Überlieferung von Johannes dem Täufer," *JBL* LI (1932), pp. 311–317, and independently K. Grobel, "He that cometh after me," *JBL* LX (1941), pp. 397–401.

16. For the several meaning of the verb "to come" see G. Kittel, *Theologisches Wörterbuch* s. v. ἔρχομαι.

17. So Grundmann in G. Kittel, *op. cit.*, s. v. ἰσχύω.

18. See more recently particularly R. Otto, *The Kingdom of God and the Son of Man* (1938), pp. 176–218.

19. As a saying of John, the word appears in Mk 1:8; Mt 3:11; and Lk 3:16. As a word of the risen Lord, it appears in Acts 1:5 and 11:16. As a word of God, in modified form, it appears in Jn 1:33, *cf.* also 1:26, 31. For the modified version of the Fourth Gospel, which needs no further comment here, see R. Bultmann, *Johannesevangelium, ad. loc.* Matthew's addition of "for repentance" is exegetical. Mark's use of the Aorist, unless its function is to point a fact, and the frequent appearance of the preposition ἐν

instead of a simple instrumental dative, may reflect the original
Aramaic form of the saying. On the transfer of the saying from
John to the risen Lord see W. Michaelis, "Täufer, Jesus, Urge-
meinde," *Neutestamentliche Forschungen* II, 3 (1928), pp. 16–35.

20. See J. Wellhausen, *Evangelium Matthaei* (1904), p. 6; A. v.
Harnack, *The Sayings of Jesus* (1908), p. 2; M. Dibelius, *Johannes der Täufer*, pp. 55–59; R. Bultmann, *Geschichte*, pp. 116–117.

21. So properly E. Lohmeyer, *Johannes der Täufer*, pp. 26, 83–86;
W. Michaelis, "Täufer," p. 31; F. Büchsel, *Der Geist Gottes im
Neuen Testament* (1926), pp. 141–142.

22. So A. T. Robertson, *John the Loyal*, pp. 101–104, A. Blakiston,
John the Baptist, p. 212, and the older interpreters.

23. In the versions of the saying preserved in Acts and in the Fourth
Gospel the implied conception of the Spirit has of course changed
and become Christian. The interpretation offered here is parallel
to that of M. Goguel, *Jean Baptiste*, pp. 39–43.

24. C. M. Edsman, "Le Baptême de feu," *Acta Seminarii Neotestamentici Upsaliensis* IX (1940).

CHAPTER III.   JOHN'S PREACHING: THE EXHORTATION

1. As originally pointed out by M. Dibelius, *From Tradition to
Gospel* (1935), pp. 17, n. 1, the *kerygma* appears in Acts 2:22–
24; 3:13–15; 10:37–42a; 13:23–31; while the asociated *parenesis*
is found in 2:38–39; 3:19–20; 10:42b–43b; 13:38–39. The ready
division of the Pauline letters into didactic and hortatory sections is illustrated by the relations between Rom 1–11 and 12–15;
Gal 1–4 and 5–6; Col 1–2 and 3–4 and I. Thess 1–3 and 4–5.

2. That John used the expression "Kingdom of God" is properly
doubted by M. Dibelius, *Johannes der Täufer*, pp. 49, 136, and
M. Goguel, *Jean Baptiste*, p. 43. Repentance not only appears
as an element of John's preaching in the summary statement Mk
1:4 and its parallels (Mt 3:2 and Lk 3:3), in the word on
Abrahamic sonship (Mt 3:8, Lk 3:8) and as a Matthean addition to the word about the two baptisms (Mt 3:11), but is probably presupposed by implication at least in Jesus' word about
the Sign of Jonah (Mt 16:4 and parallels), the similarity between
John and Jonah being that both were preachers of repentance.

3. For the Biblical, Jewish and early Christian conception of repentance see G. Kittel, *Theologisches Wörterbuch* s. v. νοέω
(Behm, Würthwein), G. F. Moore, *Judaism* I (1927), pp. 507–

534, and E. Sjöberg, "Gott und die Sünder im palästinensischen Judentum," *Beiträge zur Wissenschaft von Alten und Neuen Testament* XXVII (1939).

4. *Johannes der Täufer*, pp. 67–73.

5. See the excellent statement of E. Sjöberg, "Gott und die Sünder," p. 151.

6. See G. F. Moore, *Judaism* I, p. 508.

7. The singular form, "fruit," found in Matthew is to be preferred to Luke's plural, "fruits," partly because Luke is clearly trying to improve the logic and partly because the word itself is usually collective in Aramaic.

8. See G. F. Moore, *Judaism* I, p. 530.

9. So correctly E. Lohmeyer, *Johannes der Täufer*, p. 61.

10. So E. Lohmeyer, *op. cit.*, pp. 62–63.

11. Correctly understood, the so-called "doctrine" of the merits of the fathers implies no more than that the individual Israelite may call upon the mercy of God for the sake of the forefathers. See G. F. Moore, *Judaism* I, pp. 536–545. It may, of course, have been abused, as Justin Martyr implies in *Dialogus* 140.

12. M. Goguel has made a great deal of this episode, which he derives from a special source and in which he finds a testimony to an otherwise forgotten period of collaboration between Jesus and John and to a decisive juncture in Jesus' career, when he finally broke with the Baptist (*Jean Baptiste*, pp. 86–95). The decisive juncture at least seems arbitrarily read into the narrative. There is so much in the narrative as reported that reflects the point of view of the Fourth Evangelist and serves his immediate purposes that the original intent of the tradition is difficult to determine. In all probability the story originally had to do not with the contrast between Baptist and Christian baptism but with the question why baptism was necessary for a Jew if it was not enjoined by the Law.

13. The changes made by Matthew (9:13) and Luke (5:33) in the saying are all clearly secondary, reflecting no supplementary information. The episode may, as M. Goguel suggests (*Jean Baptiste*, p. 45), belong to the period after John's imprisonment or death.

14. Since the statement that John came "neither eating nor drinking" (Mt 11:18), as interpreted above (Chapter I), does not refer to programmatic abstinence but only to the uncertainty of visible means of supply in the wilderness, it seems impossible to accept E. Lohmeyer's division of the Baptist community into three parts, (a) the rank and file who did not fast, (b) the

disciples of John who fasted and (c) John himself, who "neither ate nor drank." See *Johannes der Täufer*, pp. 114–116.

15. On fasting in Judaism see G. F. Moore, *Judaism* II, 261–262 and Strack-Billerbeck, *Kommentar* II (1924), pp. 241–244. The relevant passages in the Testaments of the Twelve Patriarchs are: Reuben 1:9f.; Simeon 3:4; Judah 15:4; 19:2 *et al.* On the relation of fasting and repentance see also E. Sjöberg, "Gott und die Sünder," pp. 158–162, 216–219.

16. The fact that Luke in 5:33 adds "and make supplications" to his rendering of Mark's statement about fasting (Mk 2:18) probably means only that he is preparing the way for 11:1. Such "bridges" are familiar features of Luke's method of composition (*cf.* 4:13 and 22:3).

17. See *e.g.* E. Sjöberg, "Gott und die Sünder," pp. 163, 218 and G. F. Moore, *Judaism* II, p. 259.

18. See above, Chapter I, note 3.

19. Père Lagrange suggests as the locus for this group of sayings a military post and a customs house at the point where the road from Jerusalem and Jericho crossed the Jordan into Peræa at Bethany (Bethabara). See his *Évangile selon Luc*, p. 110. Perhaps the association of the three sayings is quite fortuitous or perhaps they came together because in the public mind the publicans and the soldiers were the greatest potential menace to a well-orderd life under the Law.

20. *Antiquities* XVIII, 7 = §§ 240–255.

21. The full text of the narrative is given above in Chapter I, note 3.

22. On the history of the Nabatæan kingdom see more recently A. Kammerer, *Petra et la Nabatêne* (1929) and M. I. Rostovtzeff, *Caravan Cities* (1932). Recent explorations are reported by G. and A. Horsfield, "Sela-Petra, the Rock, of Edom and Nabatene," *QDAP* VII–VIII (1928–1939) and N. Glueck, "Explorations in Eastern Palestine" I–II, *AASOR* XIV–XV, XVIII–XIX (1934, 1935, 1939). Symptomatic of their penetration into regions on a level with the northern part of Palestine is their importance in free cities such as Gerasa. See my *Gerasa, City of the Decapolis* (1938), esp. pp. 36–39.

23. Josephus, *Antiquities* XVIII, 5, 1–3 = §§ 100–125.

24. Negatively, this is indicated by what we know about Machærus, which was, in effect, a fortress, not a palace. See note 25 below. Positively, it is indicated by the availability of the high dignitaries and by the statement of Mark that Antipas "heard John gladly" (Mk 6:20). The implication here is that he would have him brought in for occasional discourse, perhaps after the evening

meal, and therefore that John was imprisoned where Antipas normally lived, probably at Tiberias. Perhaps the story of the delegation sent by John to Jesus (Mt 11:2–6 = Lk 7:18–23) also presupposes incarceration in Galilee. On this story cf. below, Chapter V.

25. The inconsistency of two statements in Josephus about Antipas' control of Machærus at this time (cf. Antiquities XVIII, 5, 1, and XVIII, 5, 2 = §§ 112 and 119) derives, apparently, from a corruption of the text (cf. the edition of Naber, ad loc.) Machærus is ably described by Josephus in his Jewish War VII, 6, 1 = §§ 164–177 and was first visited by H. B. Tristram who examined its ruins and gives a sketch-map. See his The Land of Moab (1873), pp. 267–279.

26. R. Eisler, The Messiah Jesus, pp. 288–311.

27. See, in general, my article, "Olmstead's Chronology of the Life of Jesus," already referred to in Chapter I, note 24.

CHAPTER IV.   JOHN'S RITE OF BAPTISM

1. For the name "Baptizer" cf., e.g., Mk 6:14, and for "Baptist" cf., e.g., Mt 3:1. Probably the name originated among those not directly connected with the movement. Analogies are provided by the origin of the name Christians and by the modern use of colloquial Arabic Ṣubba, "Baptists," as the designation for those who call themselves Mandai, i.e. "Gnostics," and whom we commonly refer to as the Mandeans.

2. On the meaning and use of the Greek βαπτίζω see the article by Oepke in G. Kittel, Theologisches Wörterbuch, s. v. βάπτω. The correlative Aramaic ṭebal yields as its most familiar nominal derivative the term ṭebilah, which is applied to the bath cleansing the entire body from levitical impurity.

3. For a careful discussion of these details see H. G. Marsh, The Origin and Significance of New Testament Baptism (1941), pp. 75–82.

4. For the text of the passage in Josephus see above, Chapter I, note 3.

5. The following titles provide a sampling of the more recent literature on the subject of proselyte baptism: S. Zeitlin, "The Halaka in the Gospels," HUCA I (1924), esp. pp. 357–363; idem, "A Note on Baptism for Proselytes," JBL LII (1933), pp. 78–79; idem, "L'Origine de l'institution du baptême pour les proselytes," REJ XCVIII (1934), pp. 50–57; J. Starr, "The Unjewish Character of the Markan Account of John the Baptist," JBL LI (1932),

pp. 227–237; L. Finkelstein, "The Institution of Baptism for Proselytes," *JBL* LII (1933), pp. 203–211; H. H. Rowley, "Jewish Proselyte Baptism," *HUCA* XV (1940), pp. 313–334.

6. *Babylonian Talmud*, Yebamoth 47a–47b, Soncino Translation, pp. 310–316.

7. On the general procedure for the formalization of conversion see G. F. Moore, *Judaism* I, pp. 331–334, and on the admission of converts without one or another of the three elements of procedure see the opinions of Rabbi Eliezer ben Hyrcanus and Rabbi Joshua Hananiah in Yebamoth 46a (Soncino Translation, pp. 302–303). The actual evidence for initiation by ablution alone is very meager, consisting chiefly of a passage in Epictetus (*Discourses* II, 9) and of an obscure statement in the *Sibylline Oracles* (IV, 62–67). From the statement of Josephus (*Antiquities* XX, 2, 4 = §§ 41–46) that King Izates of Adiabene was admitted as a convert to Judaism without circumcision it can conceivably be inferred that he was at least given proselyte baptism.

8. The regulations for the layman's use of the *tebilah* are set forth in Lev 11–15, Num 19 and for the high-priest's use in Lev 16. On these lustrations see W. Brandt, *Die jüdischen Baptismen* (1910), pp. 19–30. H. H. Rowley ("Jewish Proselyte Baptism," p. 315) has recently spoken of the line of reasoning that derives proselyte baptism from the *tebilah* as *a priori*. The charge would be justified only if there were no visible connections between the two rites. The connections are evident in the specifications for the quantity of water to be used in both cases (not less than 40 *seah* are implied in Yebamoth 47b in the statement that only where a menstruant may perform her ablution may a proselyte or an emancipated slave perform his baptism), in the statement that an idolatress who had bathed for matrimonial purposes could also be declared a legitimate Jewess (Yebamoth 45b) and in the early discussion between Beth Hillel and Beth Shammai (Pesachim 8, 8) as to the degree of impurity involved in the natural condition of the pagan and whether seven days must or must not intervene between the convert's circumcision and his ablution. See Strack-Billerbeck, *Kommentar* I, p. 104.

9. The comparison of the proselyte and the newly-born child is found in Yebamoth 48b. The question whether the proselyte's sins were forgiven is involved in the discussion of the problem why proselytes are afflicted (*cf.* Yebamoth 48a and the statement in Gerim 2, 5).

10. J. Leipoldt, *Die urchristliche Taufe im Lichte der Religionsgeschichte* (1928), esp. p. 27.

11. See Strack-Billerbeck, *Kommentar* I, pp. 119–120, and J. Jeremias, *Jerusalem zur Zeit Jesu IIB* (1937), p. 201.

12. "Der Ursprung der Johannestaufe," *ZNTW* XXVIII (1929), pp. 312–320.

13. So clearly in Yebamoth 46a in the discussion between Rabbi Eliezer and Rabbi Joshua, both of the late first century. Rabbi Joshua, who alludes to the earlier baptism, speaks merely of the "mothers" being bathed (in the wilderness period).

14. Among recent writers on John the Baptist M. Dibelius (*Johannes der Täufer*, p. 137) and E. Lohmeyer (*Johannes der Täufer*, pp. 151–153) reject the hypothesis deriving John's rite from proselyte baptism, M. Goguel (*Jean Baptiste*, p. 290) refusing to be specific. Writers on Christian baptism, however, usually favor the derivation. So more recently J. Leipoldt (*Die urchristliche Taufe*, pp. 26–27), F. Gavin (*Jewish Antecedents of the Christian Sacraments* [1928], pp. 26–58) and H. G. Marsh (*The Origin and Significance of New Testament Baptism* [1941], pp. 56–66).

15. The basic documents of the Mandean sect have been published and translated by M. Lidzbarski under the titles: *Das Johannesbuch der Mandäer* (1915); *Mandäische Liturgien* (1920) and *Ginza, Der Schatz oder das Grosse Buch der Mandäer* (1925). For a general conspectus of the literature on the subject of the Mandeans and a brief statement of their antiquity see my article, "A Mandaic Bibliography," *JAOS* XLVI (1926), pp. 173–177. For a description of the rite of baptism as actually practiced by the Mandeans in Iraq today see the important work of E. S. Drower, *The Mandeans of Iraq and Iran* (1937), pp. 105–118.

16. See the reviews of R. Reitzenstein's *Vorgeschichte* by H. H. Schaeder in *Gnomon* V (1929), pp. 353–370, and by M. Dibelius in *Theologische Literaturzeitung* LVI (1931), coll. 128–133.

17. J. Thomas, *Le Mouvement Baptiste en Palestine et Syrie* (1935), provides nonetheless an excellent summary of the available evidence and a proper correction of my own earlier views on the relation of John the Baptist and the Mandeans. Yet I am not inclined to accept the position of H. Lietzmann deriving Mandean baptismal practice entirely from the Christian. See his "Ein Beitrag zur Mandäerfrage," *Sitzungsberichte der preussischen Akademie der Wissenschaften*, XXVII (1930), pp. 596–608. The reasons for this, I hope to be able to develop at some future time in a discussion of Mandean theogony with which the Mandean rite of baptism is intimately related.

18. See especially Robertson Smith, *Religion of the Semites*, 3. ed. (1927), pp. 166–184 and I. Scheftelowitz, "Sündentilgung durch

Wasser," *Archiv für Religionswissenschaft* XVII (1914), pp. 353–412.

19. See especially W. Brandt, *Die jüdischen Baptismen,* pp. 9–30.
20. See *Mishnah,* Yoma III, 3.
21. On these groups in general see W. Brandt, *Die jüdischen Baptismen,* pp. 48–50. The so-called Hemerobaptists are mentioned by Justin Martyr (*Dialogue* 80, 4) and Hegesippus (quoted by Eusebius, *Ecclesiastical History* IV, 22). For Bannus see Josephus, *Life* §§ 11–12 and for Essene washings Josephus, *Jewish War* II, 8, 5, 7, 12 = §§ 129, 138, 159.
22. A. Schweitzer, *The Mysticism of Paul the Apostle* (1931), pp. 227–233. See also E. Lohmeyer, *Johannes der Täufer,* pp. 146–156.
23. See above, pp. 58–63.
24. On the eschatological role of fire see in the older literature P. Volz, *Eschatologie der jüdischen Gemeinde* (1934), pp. 318–319.
25. C. M. Edsman, "Le Baptême de feu," *Acta Seminarii Neotestamentici Upsaliensis* IX (1940). Related to the idea of a river of fire as an instrument of judgment is that of a flood of fire like the flood of water in Noah's day. See P. Volz, *Eschatologie,* pp. 335–336.
26. The important passage in the *Bundahišn* reads as follows:

    The fire and the halo melt the metal of Shatvairo in the hills and the mountains, and it (the metal) remains on this earth like a river. Then all men will pass into that metal and become pure; when one is righteous, then it seems to him just as though he walks continuously in warm milk; when wicked, it seems to him as though he walks continuously in melted metal (XXX, 19–20).

    The conception is already presupposed in the *Gathas.* See for example Yasna 34:4 and in general M. N. Dhalla, *Zoroastrian Theology* (1914), p. 61. Among earlier suggestions about the influence of Iranian eschatology see especially those of W. Bousset-H. Gressmann, *Die Religion des Judentums* 3. ed. (1926), p. 503, and E. Meyer, *Ursprung und Anfänge des Christentums,* II (1921), pp. 198–199.
27. In his review of Edsman's book H. R. Willoughby has correctly called attention to the importance of what Edsman has to say about the close relation of eschatology and ritual, the relation that comes to expression in the Baptist rite. See *JBL* LXI (1942), pp. 68–69.
28. The relevant statement of Josephus, using the expression βαπτισμῷ συνιέναι is given in full above, Chapter I, note 3. Defenders of the initiatory character of John's baptism include

M. Goguel, *Jean Baptiste*, p. 16, n. 1 and p. 291, E. Lohmeyer, *Johannes der Täufer*, pp. 31, n. 3, 92, 150, and H. G. Marsh, *New Testament Baptism*, pp. 44, 64.

29. See below, pp. 165, 174–175.

30. See his *Kingdom of God and the Son of Man*, p. 77. Among others who regard John's baptism as a sacrament we may list, F. Büchsel, *Der Geist Gottes im Neuen Testament* (1926), pp. 139–141, A. Schweitzer, *Mysticism of Paul*, pp. 227–233 and R. Reitzenstein, *Vorgeschichte*, pp. 229, 287.

31. See above, p. 98. The text of the statement of Josephus is quoted in full above, Chapter I, note 3.

32. Of course the preposition "for" (εἰς) which Mark uses can express purpose and this purpose could have been taken to be fulfilled by the rite itself, as M. Dibelius (*Johannes der Täufer*, p. 58) and M. Goguel (*Jean Baptiste*, p. 43) have pointed out. Clearly Matthew in his addition to the account of Jesus' baptism (Mt 3:14–15) and the *Gospel according to the Hebrews* as quoted by Jerome (*Against Pelagius* III, 2) were disturbed by the thought that John's baptism gave remission of sin and tried to extricate Jesus from the implications of this thought. The proper interpretation of the Markan statement is suggested by the Infancy Narrative where it is said of John, that he is to give the knowledge of salvation to his people by the forgiveness of their sins, and where it is distinctly pointed out that this forgiveness comes not through a rite but "through the tender mercy of God" (Lk 1:77–78).

CHAPTER V. JOHN THE BAPTIST AND JESUS

1. See above, Chapter I, note 15.

2. This negative judgment on the historical value of the information about John the Baptist provided by the Fourth Gospel is now shared by a majority of scholars. See especially E. C. Colwell, *John Defends the Gospel*, pp. 32–39. A contrary position is taken especially by M. Goguel, *Jean Baptiste*, pp. 235–257, who believes that Jn 1 contains elements of a written Baptist source and with its help constructs a "collaborative" phase of Jesus' ministry. On this hypothesis see below, pp. 147–150.

3. On the interpretation of the episode see *e.g.* J. Wellhausen, *Evangelium Matthei*, pp. 55–56, M. Goguel, *Jean Baptiste*, pp. 63–65, E. Lohmeyer, *Johannes der Täufer*, p. 18.

4. So correctly many modern Lives of Jesus and commentaries. See

e.g. M. Goguel, *Life of Jesus* (1933), pp. 269–271 and H. D. A. Major, T. W. Manson and C. J. Wright, *Mission and Message of Jesus* (1938), pp. 23–24.

5. Jerome, *contra Pelagium* III, 2. The text is conveniently accessible in M. R. James, *Apocryphal New Testament* (1934), p. 6, whose translation is here used.

6. On the meaning of "righteousness" in Mt 3:15 see G. Kittel, *Theologisches Wörterbuch* II, p. 200 (Schrenk).

7. For a discussion of this saying giving the variant interpretations and bibliographical information on the acceptance of the interpretation here presented see G. Kittel, *Theologisches Wörterbuch* III, pp. 412–413 (Joachim Jeremias). It is quite unnecessary in defending the interpretation offered to assume any textual confusion of the names Jonah and John.

8. On the assumption that the adversative clause about the "least in the Kingdom" is a Christian addition to the saying of Jesus see *e.g.* M. Dibelius, *Johannes der Täufer*, pp. I, 6–12; R. Bultmann, *Geschichte*, pp. 177–178; E. Lohmeyer, *Johannes der Täufer*, p. 19.

9. *Mechiltha*, ed. J. Winter and A. Wünsche (1909), pp. 77–78.

10. So the Samaritan who promises to reveal the whereabouts of the sacred cult objects missing since the days of Moses (*Antiquities* XVIII, 4, 1 = §§ 85–87), Theudas who promised that the waters of the Jordan would divide themselves as in the days of Joshua (*ibid.* XX, 5, 1 = §§ 97–98) and the Egyptian who assured his followers that at his command the walls of Jerusalem would fall down like those of Jericho (*ibid.* XX, 8, 6 = §§ 167–172 and *Jewish War* II, 13, 5 = §§ 261–263).

11. On the relevant aspects of the interpretation of this very difficult passage see *e.g.* M. Dibelius, *Johannes der Täufer*, pp. 30–31, and E. Lohmeyer, *Johannes der Täufer*, p. 17.

12. See M. Dibelius, *Johannes der Täufer*, p. 32.

13. See G. F. Moore, *Judaism* I, p. 240, and L. Ginzberg, *Legends of the Jews* VI (1939), n. 36, p. 442.

14. I Maccabees 4:44–46.

15. See above, note 2.

16. Among the many discussions of this important and difficult word see especially A. von Harnack, "Zwei Worte Jesu," *Sitzungsberichte der Akademie der Wissenschaften zu Berlin* (1907), pp. 947–957; M. Dibelius, *Johannes der Täufer*, pp. 24–29; E. Lohmeyer, *Johannes der Täufer*, pp. 113–114; H. D. A. Major, T. W. Manson and C. J. Wright, *Mission and Message of Jesus* (1938), p. 426; A. N. Wilder, *Eschatology and Ethics in the*

Teaching of Jesus (1939), pp. 175–176, and G. Kittel, *Theologisches Wörterbuch* I, pp. 608–612 (Schrenk).

CHAPTER VI. THE LATER HISTORY OF THE BAPTIST MOVEMENT

1. See the article, "Was Jesus accused of Necromancy," quoted above, Chapter I, note 12.
2. See above, pp. 156–157.
3. The text of the passage is quoted in full in Chapter I, note 3.
4. On the matter of discipleship see the article of Rengstorf in G. Kittel, *Theologisches Wörterbuch* IV, especially pp. 434–443.
5. See above, pp. 20–21.
6. See particularly the article by H. Gunkel, "Die Lieder der Kindheitsgeschichte Jesu bei Lukas," *Festgabe, A. von Harnack* (1921), and the unpublished Yale dissertation of Lucetta Mowry, *Early Christian Poetry*.
7. A. von Harnack, "Das Magnificat der Elisabet nebst einigen Bemerkungen zu Luc. 1 und 2," *Sitzungsberichte der kgl. preuss. Akademie der Wissenschaften zu Berlin* (1900), pp. 538–556. The suggestion has been accepted by not a few New Testament scholars.
8. The association of the Spirit and baptism begins to make itself felt in the narrative that tells of Peter and John's missionary work in Samaria (Acts 8:14–25) and in the story of the conversion of Cornelius (Acts 10:44–48), where those who have been baptized by other agents receive the Spirit from the hands of the recognized apostles and one who has received the Spirit is for that reason also admitted to baptism. The episodes, since they have to do with activity of Peter outside of Jerusalem, should apparently be assigned to the period following the "persecution" of the Christians by Herod Agrippa, when finally the Apostles were forced to leave the city (Acts 12:1–19). This involves a correction in the order of events as narrated by Acts and would assign the episodes to the period after 42 A.D. The conception of the Christian community as the Ecclesia and hence as the Biblical *kahal* and *'edah* is already presupposed in the Pauline theology.
9. See above, p. 54.
10. See above, pp. 156–157.
11. See above, p. 138.
12. Too much has been made in this connection of the passage Acts

19:1–7 about the "disciples" at Ephesus who had been baptized
with "John's baptism" and did not know of the existence of the
Holy Spirit. The interpreter of the passage has two options, to
emphasize the baptism of John or to emphasize the statement
that the people at Ephesus were disciples. We prefer the latter
and suggest that the people were Christians but had received
only the earliest form of Christian baptism, which did not itself
confer the Spirit. To this earlier form the designation "baptism
of John" could well have been applied by the Christians of the
late first century.

13. A full account of all the references to the use of baptismal rites
in syncretistic and Gnostic circles is given by J. Thomas, *Le
Mouvement Baptiste en Palestine et Syrie* (1935).

14. Hippolytus, *Panarion*, VI, 4 and 11.

15. See in general T. Zahn, *Geschichte des neutestamentlichen
Kanons* II (1890), especially pp. 292, 300 and A. Berendts, "Die
handschriftliche Überlieferung der Zacharias und Johannes-apo-
kryphen," *Texte u. Untersuchungen* XXVI, 3 (1904). For the
Armenian apocrypha see E. Michel and P. Peeters, *Évangiles
apocryphes* II (1914) in *Textes et Documents*, ed. H. Hemmer
and P. Lejay. Among the Coptic apocrypha see the fragments
of the *Gospel of the Twelve Apostles, Patrologia Orientalis* IX
(1913), pp. 135–139. For Syriac materials see in addition to the
Life of John (above, Chapter I, note 11) the *History of John
the Baptist, Patrologia Orientalis* IV (1908), pp. 521–541 (Greek
text of a work written in Syria in the fifth century), the
Pleophoria of John Rufus, *Patrologia Orientalis* VIII (1912), pp.
157–159, and hymns such as those of Severus of Antioch, *Patrologia Orientalis* VI (1910), pp. 163–166, and Jacob of Serug,
Zeitschrift der deutschen morgenländischen Gesellschaft XIII
(1859), pp. 46 ff. For Byzantine theologians see for instance the
homily of Theophanis Cerameus, *Patrologia Graeca* CXXXII,
col. 1061. For the survival of legends about John in the Near
East see St. H. Stephan, "Evliya Tshelebi's Travels in Palestine,"
QDAP VI (1936), p. 61, and J. W. Crowfoot, *Churches at Bosra
and Samaria, British School of Archeology in Jerusalem*, Supplementary Paper 4 (1937), p. 24.

16. On R. Eisler's hypothesis see above, Chapter I, note 4. The
relevant parts of the "Slavonic" Josephus are conveniently accessible in the Appendix to Thackeray's edition of Josephus
(Loeb Classical Library), III (1928), pp. 644–648. For a discussion of Eisler's interpretation see the review of his book by
H. Lewy, *Deutsche Literaturzeitung* III, 1, 11 (March 15, 1930),

coll. 491–492, and S. Zeitlin, *Josephus on Jesus* (1931), pp. 21–60, Most New Testament scholars reject the value of the "Slavonic" material. So M. Dibelius, *Johannes der Täufer*, pp. 127–129; M. Goguel, *Jean Baptiste*, pp. 20–33; E. Lohmeyer, *Johannes der Täufer*, pp. 31–36. The "Slavonic" Josephus is probably a Russian version of a Byzantine form of the extant Greek *Jewish War* enriched with materials from the Hebrew Josippon, Hegesippus and pious imagination.

17. On the Mandean literature see above, Chapter IV, note 15.

Subject Index

Abraham, pp. 46, 71–74, 76, 103–104, 120, 136, 149, 153, 163, 168

Ænon (near Salim), pp. 9–10, 96

Anti-Baptist polemic, pp. 128, 179

Antipas, see Herod

Aretas IV, pp. 84–89, 93, 161

Augustan era, p. 2

Bannus, p. 112

Baptism, Christian, pp. 95–96, 98–99, 105, 174–175

Baptism, John's, pp. 47, 75–76, 95–122

Baptist, see John

Baptist circles, pp. 18, 20–23, 76, 126, 159, 161, 181

Beelzebub, pp. 11–12, 61

Bethany beyond Jordan, pp. 8–9, 10

Bundahišn, p. 117

Byzantine writers on John, pp. 184–185

Christian Church, pp. 110, 123, 128, 171–176

Christian circles, pp. 62, 126

Coming One, pp. 124, 129

Crowds, word to the, pp. 36, 66, 81–83

Demons, pp. 11–12, 28–29

Disciples, Baptist, pp. 5–6, 76, 78, 119, 128, 130, 161–166, 169, 171–175

Disciples, Jesus', pp. 77–78, 135, 160, 162–164, 171–173

Disciple and master, p. 55

Disciples at Ephesus, pp. 58–59

Edsman, C. M., pp. 63, 116–117

Egyptian (Acts 21), p. 140

Eisler, R., pp. 93, 185

Elijah, pp. 12, 14, 15, 83, 92, 141–145, 159, 180–181

Elisabeth, pp. 17–18, 125–126, 170, 177

Ephesus, see disciples at

Essenes, pp. 108–109, 112, 163

Fasting, pp. 76–78, 163–164, 173–174

Fire of judgment, pp. 42, 58–63, 115–117

Fraternization (Baptist and Christian), pp. 6, 171–175

Goguel, M., pp. 147–150

Gospel, the, pp. 65–66

Harnack, A. von, p. 169

Hemerobaptists, p. 112

Herod Antipas, pp. 9, 38, 67, 83–93, 142–143, 158–159

Herod the Great, pp. 15, 24

Herodians, pp. 2, 151, 158

History, meaning, pp. 38, 45, 51

Holy People, p. 2

Holy Spirit, pp. 17, 58–61, 99, 116, 176

Honey, wild, pp. 10–11, 13

Hymnody, Baptist, pp. 166–171, 175

Immersion, pp. 97, 100, 106, 113

211

SUBJECT INDEX

Scripture References

215

SCRIPTURE REFERENCES

SCRIPTURE REFERENCES